Out *of the* Bottle

Easy and delicious recipes for making and using your own preserves

SALLY WISE

ABC
Books

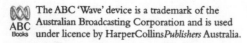 The ABC 'Wave' device is a trademark of the
Australian Broadcasting Corporation and is used
under licence by HarperCollins*Publishers* Australia.

First published in Australia in 2010
by HarperCollins*Publishers* Australia Pty Limited
ABN 36 009 913 517
harpercollins.com.au

HarperCollins*Publishers*
Level 13, 201 Elizabeth Street, Sydney NSW 2000, Australia
Unit D1, 63 Apollo Drive, Rosedale, Auckland 0632, New Zealand
A 53, Sector 57 Noida, India
77–85 Fulham Palace Road, London W6 8JB, United Kingdom
2 Bloor Street East, 20th floor, Toronto, Ontario M4W 1A8, Canada
195 Broadway NY, NY 10007

National Library of Australia Cataloguing-in-Publication data:

Wise, Sally.
  Out of the bottle: easy and delicious recipes for making and
  using home preserves / Sally Wise.
  ISBN: 978 0 7333 2557 1 (pbk.)
  Includes index.
  Condiments. Jam. Canning and preserving.
  641.852

Cover iamges: cherry jam in jar and on spoon by Alkèmia/Stock Food Gmb H; background
bowl of cherries by Photos India/PhotoLibrary.com (RF); tablecloth by istockphoto.com
Cover design by Nadia Backovic Designs
Typeset in 13.5 on 17pt Centaur by Kirby Jones
Printed and bound in Australia by McPherson's Printing Group
The papers used by HarperCollins in the manufacture of this book are a natural,
recyclable product made from wood grown in sustainable plantation forests. The fibre
source and manufacturing processes meet recognised international environmental
standards, and carry certification.

*This book is dedicated to my family who have endured my passion
for cookery over so very many years.*

In this book if a recipe states an oven temperature, it is for a fan-forced oven. If your oven is not fan-assisted or fan-forced, increase the temperature by 20°C (70°F).

CONTENTS

INTRODUCTION

It has been observed for many years that there appeared to be a lull in the time-honoured practice of preserving. Perhaps we became confident about living in a time of plenty, in a world where fresh produce of any description could be accessed at almost any time of year. Jams, pickles and tins of fruit abound on supermarket shelves, so why would we bother to make our own? Preserving continued mainly for stalwarts like me, who truly valued the flavours of home preserves and knew of their superiority over the store-bought equivalents.

In more recent times, however, there has been a rekindling of interest in preserving. Perhaps this relates to the fact that we are looking more closely at our food and raising questions about where and how the produce was grown; how far it has travelled before reaching our table; if and which chemicals were used to promote growth, deter pests and lengthen shelf life; and more importantly, what is the effect of all these factors on our health?

Many people express concern over the additives that are included in commercial products and are alarmed at their representative numbers listed on labels. We hear reports that such additives may detrimentally affect children's behaviour, and ponder the potential ramifications on our long-term health.

We are encouraged wherever possible to grow our own produce and ensure maximum nutrition through organic gardening to reduce the number of additives seeping into our diets. Yet we may not have the time, space or circumstance to grow our own. In this case, it is relatively easy to purchase good quality produce quite inexpensively when fruit and vegetables are in local seasonal abundance. It is here that preserving sits very comfortably. Through the simple process of preserving, artificial additives can be almost, if not entirely, eliminated. The produce is preserved merely by the balance of ingredients in the bottle and the methods you use to preserve them.

Having said that, preserving is about so much more than just the preparation of food—it is also easy and so much fun. It is a catalyst to communication between generations and cultures. Children love being involved, and there is the admirable side benefit that they absorb the principles of science, maths and language while they help. In turn, they come to have an appreciation for food and how it works. Best of all, they have something to share with others.

A sense of community surrounds preserving more than almost any other type of cooking. In times of large fruit and vegetable harvests, it is customary in many cultures for people to get together to jam, pickle and preserve. Even within our own society, almost every family would have its recollections of grandmothers' kitchens being filled with the aroma of jams and pickles cooking on the stove. Although the work seemed to be intensive, the memories are invariably connected to good times with family and fun with food; a sense of pride and achievement as glistening bottles were lifted from the preserver; an assurance of plenty over the months ahead.

But where can we find the time in our busy lives nowadays?

Preserving today does not need to be as labour intensive and time consuming as it was for our forebears. At our disposal we have a whole range of labour-saving devices—dishwashers, freezers, food processors, microwaves, electric preservers and dehydrators to name but a few. How our grandmothers would have envied us! These alone make preserving a far easier process. For instance, if I receive a huge amount of tomatoes, I will usually bottle some immediately, but may well choose to freeze most of them until I have the time, need or inclination to make them into a sauce or chutney.

Family size is generally smaller these days, too. In my case, as our six children gradually left home and I returned to the workforce, my time at home was much reduced. So I decided I'd make up smaller batches of preserves. Quite by accident I found that the time necessary to make jams, jellies and even chutneys and relishes was correspondingly much reduced, with the unexpected benefit of having flavours that remained sharper and more intense through the shorter boiling times. This caused a mini revolution in our household—I was able to continue preserving, to which I had become seriously addicted, and the recipes developed at this time formed the foundation for *A Year in a Bottle*.

I have increasingly come to realise that while preserves are sensational as stand-alone products, this is merely tapping into the surface of their potential—a jam can be far more than an accompaniment to scones and cream, and a pickle is far more than a mere friend to meats or cheese. A simple dish can be turned into something exceptional by the addition of a spoonful or two of the home-preserved product. It is this hidden quality that often goes unrecognised. Yet this is the major reason why my pantry shelves are lined with dozens of bottles of preserves each year—a veritable storehouse and toolbox from which to create sensational dishes.

This was the motivation for compiling *Out of the Bottle*. It contains excerpts from *A Year in a Bottle* regarding basic methods for the novice home preserver; however, its primary focus is on how to use your home preserves. It also includes a collection of over twenty-five of my favourite preserving recipes and the dishes in which they play an integral part.

For each preserve there is a minimum of four recipes. These recipes have been developed over a lifetime of experimentation. They range from the nostalgic to the more nouveau, and can be used in the home or extended into the entertaining context. A focus on flavour, ease of preparation and natural ingredients, as well as economy of cost, time and effort remains.

For my part, working and playing with food in the kitchen alongside my children has undoubtedly been the best time of my life. To this day, my family is bound together by our cooking culture, exchanging recipes almost daily and sharing our discoveries with food. It is about more than mere sustenance and nutrition—it is a force that binds us together and leaves a legacy for the future in an appreciation for food, its preservation and beyond.

GENERAL
HELPFUL
HINTS

STERILISING JARS AND BOTTLES

It is essential that preserving jars and bottles are sterilised before any products are poured into them. A simple method for doing this is as follows:

- Wash the bottles and lids in hot soapy water, rinse and place upside down on a clean cloth or dish drainer to drain.
- Place on a tray in a cold oven.
- Turn the oven to 110°C (225°F/gas ½). When the oven reaches this temperature, turn off the heat and leave the bottles for 10 minutes.
- When cooled to warm, they are ready to pour in your jam, jelly, cordial or pickles.
- Simmer lids in boiling water for 2 minutes, then drain. Dry the lids by turning them inside up on a clean towel. (If necessary, dry off any remaining water with a hairdryer.)
- To sterilise muslin for jellies, cordials and the like, place in a small saucepan, cover with boiling water and simmer for 2 minutes. Allow to cool to lukewarm before handling.

JAMS, JELLIES, FRUIT CHEESES AND PASTES

There is a natural substance in fruit called pectin which, when boiled with the correct amount of sugar and sufficient acid, reacts to form a gel. This is the building block for jams, jellies, fruit cheeses and pastes.

Jams are thick and soft spreads made by boiling fruit and sugar (often with lemon juice added). When making jam it is important to use the freshest fruit. Produce that has been sitting on the shelves for a considerable time has less chance of making good preserves. Using the freshest produce means there is far less risk of spoilage. It is very disappointing to go to the trouble of making a lovely batch of preserves, only to find they have quite soon gone mouldy and need to be discarded.

Conserves are similar to jams in consistency, but usually contain more defined pieces of fruit in the finished product. Conserves are generally made by layering the prepared raw fruit with the sugar and mixing gently. The mixture is left to stand overnight, after which lemon juice is added and the mixture boiled to the setting point as for jam.

Jellies are clear fruit, sugar and acid (usually lemon juice) mixtures that are cooked until a gel is formed, which is tender but firm enough to hold its shape.

Fruit pastes or butters are spreads made from fruit, sugar, a little water and usually a small amount of lemon juice.

Fruit cheeses contain the same ingredients as fruit pastes but are cooked for longer to form a cheese-like consistency.

It is recommended that jams, jellies, fruit cheeses and butters, as well as cordials, contain 60 per cent sugar to the weight of the fruit. That is, for each kilogram of fruit, a minimum of 600g (1lb 5oz) of sugar should be used for effective preservation.

In order to better understand the central role of pectin, I've included some extra information that may be helpful.

Facts about pectin

Several factors can assist in maximising pectin in the jam you are making:

- Use fruit that is just slightly under-ripe.
- Don't use fruit that is very ripe—save this for relish or chutney (even then, not too ripe).
- Use fruit that has only recently been picked. Pectin levels drop significantly the longer the fruit has been on the shelf.
- Freezing fruit lowers the pectin level.
- Combine a fruit with low pectin levels with one that is high in pectin (see table opposite for Testing for pectin levels in fruit).
- Acid assists in the release of pectin. For this reason it

is important to add lemon juice or citric acid from the outset.

❖ Keep in mind that the amount of pectin can vary with the season. For example, in a wet season blackberries (and other berry fruits) contain more moisture, which results in less pectin per volume of fruit.

Following is a simple test to ascertain if the pectin levels in the fruit you are using are sufficient:

❖ Simmer the fruit with a little water until it is soft.

❖ Place 1 teaspoon of the fruit juice from this mixture in a heatproof glass.

❖ When cool, add 3 teaspoons of methylated spirits and shake gently. Leave to stand for 1 minute. A translucent jelly-like substance will have formed.

The following table will give an indication of the results and how to match these to the proportion of sugar that should be used.

Testing for pectin levels in fruit

Evidence (jelly-like clot)	Pectin level	Quantity of fruit pulp	Quantity of sugar
1 firm clot	High	1kg (2lb 4oz)	1.25kg (2lb 12 oz)
2–3 less firm clots	Medium	1kg (2lb 4oz)	1kg (2lb 4oz)
Many small clots	Poor	1kg (2lb 4oz)	750g (1lb 10oz)

The table below gives an indication of pectin levels of many of the fruit used in jams and preserves.

Fruit pectin levels

Poor	Medium	High
Cherries	Apricots	Currants (red, black, white)
Strawberries	Blackberries	Damsons
Pears	Greengages	Cranberries
Elderberries	Loganberries	Citrus fruits
Figs	Raspberries	Quinces
Mulberries	Plums (most varieties)	Crab-apples
Rhubarb	Peaches	
Nectarines	Blueberries	
Medlars	Grapes	
Kiwi fruit	Tomatoes	
Mangoes	Eating apples	
Melons	Persimmons	
Pineapples		
Passionfruit		
Bananas		
Guavas		

At times it may be advantageous to add pectin to jams and jellies made from fruit with low pectin levels. In this case a liquid pectin stock can be prepared as follows.

PECTIN STOCK

1kg (2lb 4oz) gooseberries, white currants, crab-apples or
cooking apples (such as Granny Smiths)
3 cups water

Combine the gooseberries, white currants or apples (or even just the cores) and water in a large saucepan over medium heat. Bring to the boil and simmer for 45 minutes. Strain through a colander, then strain the resulting liquid through a double thickness of muslin. Use in the proportions listed in the table below. Freeze any excess pectin stock in small containers.

Makes 4 cups

Note: *Alternatively, commercial pectin powder may be added. Recommended quantities are outlined in the following table.*

Adding pectin to jams and jellies

Fruit	Liquid pectin stock	Commercial pectin powder
1kg (2lb 4oz)	1 cup	15g (½ oz)

As more commercial varieties of pectin for jam become available, it may be wise to check the packet for recommended amounts, as some are stronger than others.

Note: *Keep in mind that adding too much pectin will give the jam or jelly a dull and uninteresting flavour, so use sparingly. An alternative is to combine a low-pectin fruit with a high-pectin fruit, as in the case of mulberry jam or mulberry jelly, where cooking apples are added to increase the pectin levels.*

Acid content

As I've already mentioned, it is important that acid levels in the fruit are sufficient for optimum setting of the jam, jelly, paste or cheese. Types of fruit that are low in acid include strawberries, pears, sweet varieties of cherry, figs, kiwi fruit, mangoes, melons, pineapples and tomatoes. When using low-acid fruit it is advisable to add at the outset 2 tablespoons of lemon juice or 1 level teaspoon of citric acid to each 2kg (4lb 8oz).

An alternative is to combine these types of fruit with a high-acid fruit, for example, melon and lemon jam.

Testing for set in jams and jellies

There are three main methods for testing for set:

- **Insert a sugar thermometer in the mixture.** When the mixture reaches 105°C (220°F), the sugar reacts with the fruit and acid to form the pectin gel, which means that the setting point has been reached.
- **Flake test.** Collect a small amount of the mixture with a metal spoon. Allow to cool a little, then tilt the spoon on its side. If the jam is ready it will fall from the spoon in a sheet, rather than in liquid drops.
- **Wrinkle test.** Place 2 teaspoons of the mixture on a cold saucer and transfer to the fridge for a few minutes. Run your finger through the cold jam; if the surface is quite firm and wrinkles when you pull your finger through it, the jam has reached setting point.

Sugar-free jams

Many people request recipes for sugar-free jams. This may be for health reasons, such as diabetes, or personal preference. Sugar-free jams do not keep well as they contain little or no sugar, and sugar in jams is an important preserving agent. Some recipes containing no sugar at all utilise artificial sweetener instead. With such recipes, it is really important to remember not to add the artificial sweetener while the mixture is hot as it takes on an unpleasant metallic taste. The jam should be kept in the fridge for no longer than 2 weeks.

I once read a recipe that used glycerine instead of artificial sweetener. I haven't tried this but for what it's worth, the amount to use is 90g (3¼oz) glycerine to 500g (1lb 2oz) fruit.

Other recipes call for a combination of fruit for a sweeter taste, and a lesser amount of sugar—raspberry and apple jam is an example of this. Again, these jams will not keep for as long as those with 60 per cent or more sugar, so they also should be kept refrigerated for up to 2 weeks.

RASPBERRY AND APPLE JAM

—⌐

250g (9oz) raspberries
250g (9oz) peeled, cored and diced cooking apple
   (such as Granny Smiths)
½ cup sugar
1 tablespoon commercial pectin powder

Place the raspberries in a saucepan over medium heat and cook until the juices start to flow. Add the apple and simmer for 10 minutes, or until soft, stirring occasionally.

Combine the sugar and pectin powder in a small bowl and mix well. Stir into the simmering fruit. Bring to the boil, stirring occasionally, and cook for 10 minutes.

Pour into warm sterilised jars and seal immediately. Keep, stored in the fridge, for up to 2 weeks.

Makes approximately 300g (10½oz)

Note: *Any type of berry can be used in this jam.*

SUGAR-FREE BERRY JAM

The types of berry that could be used in this jam include raspberry, blackberry, loganberry, strawberry, silvanberry, youngberry and tayberry.

1kg (2lb 4oz) berries
½ cup water
juice of ½ lemon
25g (1oz) commercial pectin powder
4 teaspoons liquid artificial sweetener, or to taste

Place the berries, water and lemon juice in a large saucepan over medium heat and bring to the boil. Reduce the heat to low and cook for 15 minutes, stirring often. Remove from the heat and stir in the pectin powder. Bring back to the boil and cook for a further 10 minutes. Allow to cool to lukewarm, then add the artificial sweetener and mix well.

Pour into warm sterilised jars and seal. Turn upside down and leave to stand for 2 minutes, then turn right way up. Store in the fridge and use within 2 weeks.

Makes approximately 700g (1lb 9oz)

Sugar-free Stone Fruit Jam

Peaches, apricots, nectarines and plums are suitable for this recipe.

> 1kg (2lb 4oz) stone fruit, halved and stones removed,
>   chopped
> ½ cup water
> juice of ½ lemon
> 3 teaspoons commercial pectin powder
> 3 teaspoons liquid artificial sweetener, or to taste

Place the fruit, water and lemon juice in a large saucepan over medium heat and bring to the boil. Reduce the heat to low and cook for 20 minutes, stirring often. Remove from the heat and stir in the pectin powder. Bring back to the boil and cook for a further 10 minutes. Set aside and allow to cool to lukewarm. Add the artificial sweetener and mix well.

Pour into warm sterilised jars and seal. Turn jars upside down and leave to stand for 2 minutes, then turn right way up. Keep in the fridge and use within 2 weeks.

Makes approximately 700g (1lb 9oz)

Marmalades

Marmalades are simple and economical to make. They are delightful used as a spread on toast or as a topping for a steamed pudding.

If adding alcohol to marmalade, the amount to use is 2 tablespoons to 500g (1lb 2oz) of completed marmalade.

Pectin levels diminish with the progression of the citrus season, so the table below may be helpful.

Tips for marmalade quantities

	Early in season	Late in season
Fruit	500g (1lb 2oz)	500g (1lb 2oz)
Water	6 cups	3 cups
Sugar	2kg (4lb 8oz)	1kg (2lb 4oz)

CHUTNEYS, RELISHES AND PICKLES

Chutneys are generally cooked for 1–4 hours. They are made from finely sliced or chopped fruit and vegetables that are cooked very slowly until smooth in texture and rounded in flavour.

Relishes are cooked for a shorter amount of time than chutneys. The end product is chunkier and the flavour is often sharper.

Clear pickles are fruit and/or vegetables that have been brined, then covered in spiced or flavoured vinegar.

Brining is important to pickling. The salt in the brine helps slow down the growth of bacteria and extracts moisture so that the vinegar solution can penetrate the fruit or vegetables.

When pickles, such as pickled onions, are first placed in bottles, they may not remain submerged in the vinegar solution. If this happens, the uncovered fruit or vegetables may spoil. In order to correct this, place a piece of crumpled baking paper in the top of the jar, pressing it down into the liquid. Leave for 1–2 weeks, after which the paper can be removed and the fruit or vegetables should stay submerged. If they don't, repeat this process with a fresh piece of baking paper.

EQUIPMENT AND INGREDIENTS

Equipment for making preserves

- 4–6 litre (140–210fl oz) heavy-based stainless steel saucepan
- long-handled wooden and large metal spoons
- cook's knife
- paring knife
- heatproof jug for pouring jam into jars
- jam jars—recycled is fine, as long as they are scrupulously clean and heatproof
- muslin—can be purchased from fabric stores and speciality kitchen stores
- 18 x 28 x 3cm (7 x 11¼ x 1¼in) tray for fruit cheeses
- 25 x 30 x 5cm (10 x 12 x 2in) Swiss roll tin

Equipment for preserving fruit

- a preserving outfit if at all possible
- preserving jars with, in some cases, rubber rings and metal lids and clips, or screw-top jars especially designed for bottling fruit (available from speciality kitchen stores and good bottle and jar suppliers)

Equipment for cooking

- whisks—stainless steel, one small and one large
- heatproof mixing bowls—small, large and medium
- graters—coarse and fine
- sieves—small and large
- electric beaters
- food mill
- heavy-based saucepans and frying pans
- wire racks
- silicone spatulas—firm and soft
- food processor or hand-held stick blender
- mortar and pestle
- spice grinder or coffee grinder
- chopping boards—separate wooden and/or plastic boards are best for preparing different foods, for example, meats (raw), meats (cooked), poultry, seafood, vegetable, dairy and fruit, to avoid any risk of cross-contamination
- scales—for weighing ingredients, electronic scales are the most accurate
- measuring cups and measuring spoons
- rolling pin
- piping bags and nozzles
- baking tins and heatproof dishes:
  - patty pans
  - muffin tins
  - 18 x 28cm (7 x 11¼in) slab tin and 25 x 30 x 3cm (10 x 12 x 1¼in) Swiss roll tin

- baking trays
- 20cm (8in) round cake tin
- 20cm (8in) springform cake tin
- I-litre (35fl oz) and 2-litre (70fl oz) flameproof casserole dishes
- 20cm (8in) pie dish
- 18cm (7in) pie dish
- I-cup capacity pie dishes or ramekins

Handy ingredients

- ❖ cooking spray
- ❖ frozen puff pastry sheets—it is simply too time consuming to make your own
- ❖ tomato sauce—rarely used but a handy back up if you run out of the homemade product
- ❖ soy sauce
- ❖ Worcestershire sauce
- ❖ stock powder
- ❖ cornflour—maize cornflour is best
- ❖ vinegar—white, white wine or cider
- ❖ custard powder
- ❖ cocoa powder
- ❖ vanilla essence or extract
- ❖ tinned tomatoes
- ❖ tomato paste

HARD-WON HINTS

Cooking should be fun, never tedious, so I've tried to eliminate any unnecessary steps in recipes. If a recipe can't tolerate this level of off-handedness, then it's not the one for me. These hints are about simplifying the cooking process. Purists may shudder at my suggestions, but they have worked for me over the years.

Breadcrumbs

Fresh breadcrumbs can be easily made from stale scraps of bread. This is where a food processor or blender is invaluable. Place small pieces of bread into the bowl of the food processor and process into crumbs. These can then be frozen, if you have an excess, for later use.

Eggs

Left-over egg whites can be frozen in small airtight containers and used later in pavlovas or meringue nests. To thaw, leave in the fridge.

Some recipes in this book call for brushing a pastry base with egg white. There is no need to use a fresh egg. If you are doing other baking at the time, keep the egg shell and simply use a pastry brush to scrape out the residual egg white in the shell.

Left-over egg yolks can be used in place of some of the whole eggs in quiches, egg and bacon pies or green eggs and ham pie. Egg yolk can also be used to seal pastry before baking.

If you want to check if an egg is fresh, place it in a bowl of cold water. If it floats, throw it out.

Grating

To reduce the chance of food sticking to the grater, run the grater under water before grating citrus zest or cheese or spray with cooking oil.

Measuring

If you're using the measuring jug for something else, a handy alternative for measuring small amounts of liquid is a baby's bottle. A few handy conversions are as follows:

I cup butter = 250g (9oz)
I cup of liquid = 250ml (9fl oz)
I dessertspoon = 2 teaspoons
I tablespoon = 4 teaspoons

Note: *Dry weights are not the same as liquid weights.*

Mixing

I don't fold in flour and milk alternately. It never seems to matter as long as the flour is added first, but don't mix it in until you have added the liquid.

Instead of creaming butter and sugar with a wooden spoon, use a whisk. I soften the butter in the microwave first. For 250g (9oz), about 30 seconds on MEDIUM, then in 10-second bursts if it needs a little extra. By using a whisk, you don't have to change utensils when you add eggs—less mess, less washing up.

Mixing bowls

Think about how you are doing your cooking. For instance, suppose you are making a plain butter cake as well as a chocolate cake. Deal with the plain cake first, then you don't need to wash the bowl before making the chocolate one.

Oven temperatures

In this book if a recipe states an oven temperature, it is for a fan-forced oven. If your oven is not fan-assisted or fan-forced, increase the temperature by 20°C (70°F).

Pastry

I always keep a supply of ready-rolled pastry sheets in the freezer. I'd like to say I can make good puff pastry but it wouldn't be true. The sheets are so easy to use, and low fat varieties are now readily available.

Removing rind from bacon

Use your fingernail or a small knife to make a small incision just below the hard edge of the rind, and then peel it off. It's easy to do.

Sifting

Here are my recommendations for sifting ingredients:

- ❖ Plain flour—only if the recipe specifies to do so.
- ❖ Icing sugar—only if it's lumpy.
- ❖ Self-raising flour—again I don't sift it, just make sure it's mixed together well. I always make my own (2 teaspoons of baking powder to 1 cup of plain flour.)
- ❖ Cocoa powder—only if it's lumpy.
- ❖ Ground spices—don't bother.

If you really feel you must sieve, you don't need to buy a sifter. On the exceptionally rare occasions that I do think it might be a good idea to sift, such as for a sponge cake, I use a nylon sieve and shake it about over the mixture in the bowl.

BASIC PRESERVING

The recipes in this book are cooked on the stovetop. Smaller batches, using 1kg (2lb 4oz) of fruit, can be made successfully in the microwave by placing the fruit in a microwave-safe bowl and cooking on HIGH until soft. Add the sugar, stir to dissolve and cook on HIGH until boiling and then setting point is reached (see page 18). Watch at all times. Pour the jam into sterilised jars or bottles and seal immediately.

Jams and marmalades

* Most fruit needs to be washed with the exception of very soft fruit, such as raspberries.
* Some fruit, such as apricots, peaches and nectarines, need to have stones removed.
* Place the fruit in the saucepan with the specified amount of water and lemon juice or citric acid.
* Cook, stirring occasionally, until the fruit is softened. Stir apricots more often as they tend to catch. Greasing the base of the pan helps prevent this.
* Remove the fruit mixture from the heat and stir in the sugar.

- Return to the heat and bring back to the boil, stirring to dissolve the sugar.
- Boil steadily, without stirring, until setting point is reached (see page 18).
- Remove from the heat and allow to stand in the saucepan for 10 minutes, then pour into warm sterilised jars or bottles.
- Seal immediately and store in a cool, dry, dark place.
- Refrigerate after opening.

Note: *Yields given for jams, jellies and marmalades are approximate as fruit pectin levels vary considerably. Lower pectin levels require longer cooking times which causes more evaporation and may result in less yield.*

Fruit jellies

- Prepare the fruit as for jam.
- Add the lemon juice and enough water to barely cover. Berries need much less water.
- Bring to the boil and cook until the fruit is softened and has released its juice.
- Strain through a colander, then strain the resulting liquid through a double thickness of muslin.
- To each cup of liquid, add 1 cup of sugar (the amount of sugar can be reduced to ⅔ cup if desired, particularly for lower pectin fruits).
- Return to the heat and bring to the boil, stirring to dissolve the sugar.

- Cook steadily, until setting point is reached (see page 18).
- Do not stir in any scum that rises to the surface" remove with a slotted spoon or put a few small pieces of butter on the surface to help prevent it forming in the first place.
- Remove from the heat and pour into warm sterilised jars or bottles. Seal immediately. Store in a cool, dry and dark place.
- Refrigerate after opening.

Cordials

- Place the fruit in a saucepan with the specified amount of water.
- Bring to the boil and cook until the fruit is soft.
- Strain through a colander, then strain the resulting liquid through a double thickness of muslin.
- To this liquid, add 1 cup of sugar to each cup of juice (this may vary in some recipes).
- Return to the cleaned saucepan and bring to the boil, stirring occasionally. Reduce the heat to low.
- Cook for 2 minutes, just simmering.
- At this stage some recipes add citric acid, tartaric acid or vinegar, stirring until dissolved.
- Pour into warm sterilised bottles and seal immediately. Store in a cool, dry and dark place.
- Refrigerate after opening.

Fruit pastes and cheeses

- Prepare the fruit as for jam and place in a saucepan with very little water and lemon juice.
- Cook until the fruit is very soft.
- Strain the mixture through a fine sieve or food mill.
- To each cup of fruit pulp, I generally add 1 cup of sugar unless the recipe specifies otherwise.
- Bring to the boil, stirring to dissolve the sugar.
- Cook, stirring frequently, over medium–low heat until a paste is produced. Towards the end of cooking the heat may need to be reduced to very low.
- To make a fruit cheese, the mixture should be cooked for longer. It is ready when a wooden spoon dragged through the mixture leaves a clear trail across the base of the saucepan.
- For pastes, spoon into warm sterilised jars and seal immediately. Store in a cool, dry and dark place.
- For fruit cheeses, pour the mixture into foil-lined baking tins to a depth of 1.5cm ($^5/_8$ in) and leave to set. When completely cold, cut into squares and place between layers of baking paper in an airtight container. Store in a cool, dry, dark place.

Bottling fruit

Bottling fruit in syrup, fruit juice or water is a preserving method that has been used for generations. Preserving fruit this way was originally done in enormous old-fashioned kettles, then purpose-built preserving outfits on top of fuel, and later electric, stoves. Now we have the modern-day preservers that include the welcome addition of thermostat control.

For effective preserving, it is necessary to bring the core temperature of the fruit in the bottle to 85°C (185°F) so that harmful bacteria are destroyed. Food experts recommend testing a sample jar with a food thermometer to ensure that this is the case. Inadequate heat can lead to poor sterilisation and spoilage. It is also necessary for the temperature to be held at this point for differing periods of time. This is because fruits that have lower acid levels may need longer. Greater volume needs extra time to ensure all contents of the bottle reach the required temperature.

Publications that include safe and reliable guides and provide specific instructions on times and temperatures for different types of fruit are available from suppliers of home-bottling kits. Should you choose to purchase such a kit, they are available from speciality kitchen and hardware stores. Any cost in the purchasing is quickly recouped when you actually start preserving fruit.

Fruits that are low in acid, such as tomatoes, pears, bananas, figs, melons and mangoes, need citric acid or lemon juice to be added to enhance preservation.

There are many types of bottle available nowadays (I use the Fowlers Vacola jars that I've acquired over the years from a range of sources). Take care to ensure that any jars you use are guaranteed to be heat-safe for the amount of time required for preserving. Also make sure that replacement sealing rings for bottles are readily available.

Always use fruit in premium condition and utensils that are scrupulously clean.

The actual bottling of the fruit is simple. The basic procedure I use is as follows:

- Wash the bottles, ring and lids in hot soapy water, then rinse in cool water. Drain.
- Prepare the preserving syrup of choice.
- Place the rubber rings on the bottles, making sure that the ring is not twisted.
- Prepare the fruit and pack neatly into the clean bottles.
- Fill the jar to the top with the prepared preserving syrup.
- Place the lid evenly on the jar, then secure with the clips. If using a screw-top jar, screw on the lid.
- Place the jars in the preserver.
- Fill preserver with cool water to just cover the lids.
- Follow the manufacturer's instructions or recipes in this book for the particular fruit and cook at the specified temperature for required amount of time.
- Remove from the preserver and stand on a wooden chopping board.
- Allow to stand undisturbed for 24 hours, or until completely cold.
- Remove the clips: lids should be concave. If the seal is broken, store in fridge and use within 3 days.

Note: *For many years, and still to this day, some people placed the prepared bottles of fruit (complete with lids, rings and clips) in a baking tin filled with 3cm (1¼in) water in a 180°C (350°F/gas 4) oven for 1 hour. Food authorities no longer recommend preserving in this way.*

More recently some people have found that preserving fruit in a microwave oven is effective. Food authorities do not recommend it as many factors can affect the quality of the finished product. For instance, using other appliances at the same time may interfere with the operation of the microwave. Another factor to consider is that the even distribution of heat is not always guaranteed in a microwave, which means that the core temperature of the fruit in the bottles may not reach the required 85°C (185°F).

Chutneys, pickles and relishes

- Prepare the fruit and/or vegetables according to the recipe.
- In some cases, brining the fresh produce is recommended.
- Cook for the amount of time recommended in the recipe, or until the desired consistency is reached.
- Pour into warm sterilised jars and seal immediately.
- Store in a cool, dry and dark place.
- Refrigerate after opening.

Clear pickles

- Brining the vegetables is generally recommended to extract some of the natural juices, allowing the vinegar to penetrate and preserve effectively.
- Prepare the vinegar and spice mixture.

- Generally, the method is to place the brined vegetables in sterilised jars and pour over the vinegar. Some recipes call for the vinegar to be cooled before covering the vegetables, in others it should be used hot.
- It is essential that the vegetables are submerged in the vinegar mixture. If they float to the surface, a simple remedy is to place a piece of crumpled baking paper in the top of the jars and press down into the vinegar. After a week the paper can be removed and the vegetables should remain submerged. If they don't, replace the paper and leave for another week.
- Seal immediately.
- Store in a cool, dry and dark place.
- Refrigerate after opening.

Sauces

- Use a similar method to chutneys, pickles and relishes. It is important to note that the ingredients and methods for individual recipes will result in a more liquid consistency.
- Strain the sauce into the cleaned saucepan, return to the heat and bring to the boil.
- Pour into sterilised bottles and seal immediately.
- Store in a cool, dry and dark place.
- Refrigerate after opening.

Troubleshooting chart

Product	Problem	Cause	Comments
Jam	Not setting	Too little pectin	Add lemon juice and re-boil
		Incorrect balance between pectin and acid	Add commercial pectin—15g (½oz) to 1kg (2lb 4oz) fruit mixture—or 1 cup pectin stock
		Insufficient cooking time	Cook for specified time or until setting point is reached
Jam	Too dark	Poor-quality fruit	Use fruit that is *just slightly* under-ripe for maximum pectin level, flavour and colour
		Cooked too long, so sugar has caramelised	If jam does not reach setting point within 25 minutes, add commercial pectin (see 'Adding pectin to jams and jellies' on page 17) and boil for 10 minutes more

Product	Problem	Cause	Comments
Jam	Crystallisation	Too much sugar	Refer to 'Testing for pectin levels in fruit' on page 15 for recommended quantities of sugar
		Lack of acid in fruit	Add lemon juice at outset
			Add ¼ teaspoon of cream of tartar to each 1kg (2lb 4 oz) jam, or a pinch of tartaric acid, when jam is nearly cooked
		Over-boiling	Boil only until setting point is reached
		Sugar not dissolved when mixture brought to the boil	Ensure sugar is dissolved before boiling point is reached again
			Add 30g (1oz) butter per 1kg (2lb 4oz) of fruit (after boiling for some time)
Jam	Tough fruit	Insufficient cooking before sugar was added	Taste test fruit before adding sugar
			As an alternative, use conserve method— layer sugar with fruit. Stand overnight, then cook until setting point is reached

Product	Problem	Cause	Comments
Jam	Fruit has risen	Jars too hot	Leave until completely cold, then fold fruit through evenly, top with baking paper dipped in brandy then reseal
		Jam not allowed to settle before bottling	Allow jam to stand for 10 minutes before pouring into jars
Jam	Mouldy on top	Wet or poor-quality fruit	Use fruit in good condition
		Covered while warm	Cover jam when piping hot
		Stored in a warm, unventilated and/or damp place	Place a bowl of lime on the shelf where jams are kept
		Too much water added to the mixture	See individual recipes for exact quantities
		Jars were wet	Ensure sterilised jars are completely dry
Jam	Fermented	Poor quality fruit	Discard!
		Insufficient cooking	
		Not enough sugar	
		Incorrect storage	

Product	Problem	Cause	Comments
Jelly	Cloudy	Sugar or fruit not clean	Wash fruit well, use good-quality sugar
		Jelly bag was squeezed	Don't squeeze jelly bag
		Boiled too fast as setting point was reached	If mixture rises and bubbles, reduce heat
		Jelly bag still contains some residue, or if new, some minuscule pieces of fibre from the fabric (e.g. flannel)	Wash jelly bag and scald before using
		Scum was stirred in	Remove scum from surface with slotted spoon for smaller streaks, add small knobs of butter to disperse
Jelly	Dark on surface during storage	Stored in too warm a place	Store in a cool, dry and dark place
		Stored in too light a place	
		Stored too long (this often occurs with apple and other light jellies due to enzyme action)	Carefully scoop out darker section after opening each jar for use

Product	Problem	Cause	Comments
Jelly	Thick and syrupy but not set	Insufficient pectin	Add lemon juice—1 tablespoon to 1kg (2lb 4oz)—then re-boil for 5 minutes. Alternatively, stir in commercial pectin and boil for 10 minutes more
Jelly	Set in preserving pan before bottling	Acid content too high	Combine with lower acid fruit
Jelly	White streaks	Scum stirred in	Add a few small knobs of butter to disperse small pieces of scum
		Scum not removed carefully before bottling	Remove large pieces of scum with slotted spoon
Jelly	Air bubbles	Jelly poured too slowly or too quickly into jars	Pour steadily into jars, ensuring air bubbles are not trapped
		Jelly not poured down inside surface of jar	Pour jelly down inside surface of jar
		Boiled too fast as setting point was reached	If mixture rises and bubbles, reduce heat
		Allowed to stand too long before bottling	Bottle within 5—10 minutes of cooking

Product	Problem	Cause	Comments
Jelly	Not setting in large jars	Too slow in cooling process	Use smaller even-sized, similar shaped jars
Conserve	Fruit doesn't stay whole	Fruit not mixed with sugar and left to stand long enough	Leave combined sugar and fruit to stand overnight at least
		Cooked too long	If conserve does not reach setting point within 25 minutes, add commercial pectin (see page 17 for 'Adding pectin to jams and jellies) and boil for 10 minutes more
Conserve	Shrinks in jar	Seal faulty Storage conditions too warm	Store in a cool, dark and dry place. Place freezer bag over lid and secure with a rubber band
Conserve	Air pockets	Too cool before pouring into jars	Allow to stand no more than 10 minutes before bottling
Marmalade	Cloudy	Too much pith included (this will always happen if whole fruit is minced)	Ensure pith is removed
		Scum stirred in	Remove scum with slotted spoon

Product	Problem	Cause	Comments
Marmalade	Peel rises to surface	Jars too hot when marmalade is poured into them	Allow sterilised jars to cool to warm before pouring marmalade into them
		Mixture not allowed to stand before bottling	Allow marmalade to stand for 10 minutes before bottling
Chutney	Shrinks in jar	Over-boiled	Cook only until chutney-like consistency is reached with no clear vinegar evident
		Not covered tightly enough	After bottling, place a freezer bag over lid and secure with a rubber band
		Stored in a warm place	
Chutney	Mouldy	Poor quality fruit and/or vegetables	Discard!
		Insufficient vinegar	
		Under-cooked	
		Use of unsterilised jars	
		Use of damp jars	
Chutney	Liquid on surface	Insufficient boiling down of mixture	Cook until no clear vinegar liquid is evident
Flavoured oils	Cloudy	Flavouring contains too much liquid (e.g. onions)	Use quickly or it will become rancid

Product	Problem	Cause	Comments
Flavoured oils	Rancid	Incorrect storage	Discard!
		Faulty seal on bottles	For future reference:
		Oil came into direct contact with sunlight or heat	Basil oil—remove herb from oil after 2 weeks
			Garlic oil—use within 2 weeks (keep refrigerated during this time)
Pickles	Not crunchy	Not salted long enough	Ideally soak in brine for 24 hours
		Brine too weak	**Brine (for general use)**—500g (1lb 2oz) salt to 20 cups water. Dissolve salt and use cold. Enough for 3–4kg (6lb 12oz–9lb) vegetables. Drain well
		Vinegar quantity or acetic acid level insufficient to preserve adequately	**Dry brining**—250g (9oz) salt to 750g (1lb 10oz) vegetables. Rinse and drain well
Pickles	Hollow	Raw ingredients too mature	Use freshest produce possible
		Vegetables kept too long before use	

Product	Problem	Cause	Comments
Pickles	Pale or bleached	Jar exposed to light during storage	Store in a cool, dry and dark place
Pickles	Soft and slippery	Salt or vinegar solution not strong enough	Discard!
Pickles	Dark in colour	Iodised salt used	Use cooking salt
		Too many spices	Use whole spices in a muslin bag
		Ground spices used	
		Dark vinegar used	Use white, white wine or cider vinegar
		Brine made with hard water	Use bottled or filtered water
Pickles	Vegetables or fruit rise to top	Vinegar takes a little time to penetrate vegetables	Place a piece of crumpled baking paper in jar, leave for 1 week, remove. Repeat if necessary
Pickles	Garlic looks green	Caused by a reaction with the vinegar	Blanch garlic before use
Pickles	Green spots on pickled onions	Caused by fermentation of a harmless substance	Okay to eat. I remove the outer spotted layer as often the rest of the onion is unaffected

Product	Problem	Cause	Comments
Pickles	Unpleasant odour	Pickles are spoiled	Discard!
Pickles	Fermented or mould visible	Too little sugar	Discard!
		Cooking time too short	
		Brine or vinegar solution too weak	
		Cooking equipment not clean	
		Incorrect storage	
		Decayed or bruised fruit/vegetables used	
Sauce	Separation on storage	May not have been cooked long enough so that it still has a watery appearance	Cook sauce down until no clear vinegar liquid is evident
		Tomato sauce—breaking down of pectin gel	Shake to restore smoothness
Sauce	Dark on top	Tomato sauce is susceptible to this—lids may not have been airtight	Cover lid with a small freezer bag, secure with a rubber band or dip completed bottles in sealing wax

DEHYDRATING

Dehydrating food is an excellent way to process fruit, vegetables, herbs and spices and even meat. This form of preservation removes moisture from food so that the growth of bacteria, yeast and mould is inhibited and the enzyme action that causes foods to spoil is slowed down. Any produce that is to be dehydrated should be very fresh and of the highest possible quality.

Three primary methods can be employed: oven drying, the use of a dehydrator and sun drying. Sun drying can be a little tricky sometimes—a humid climate is not really conducive to sun drying)—so only the first two methods will be discussed here.

When using the oven drying method, the temperature needs to be a steady 60–70°C (140–150°F/gas ¼) to be effective. The purchase of an oven thermometer is highly recommended to ensure that the temperature remains consistent at all times. The oven door should be left just slightly ajar, or opened briefly occasionally to allow moisture to escape. The food on the baking trays should be rotated to ensure even dehydration of the entire batch.

A food dehydrator is a good investment as it allows the temperature to be controlled easily. Specific temperatures and times are provided by the manufacturers for different types of food.

Dehydrated food should be cooled, then tightly packed and placed in airtight containers, such as small glass jars, plastic containers with-tight fitting lids or freezer bags.

Store dehydrated food in a cool, dry and dark place. For safety's sake, I store these containers in the fridge and if it is not to be used within 3 weeks, in the freezer. As another safety measure, check the dehydrated food occasionally. If there is any sign of mould growing on the food, throw it out immediately as it is not at all safe to eat.

FRUIT

Some types of fruit, such as cherries, blueberries, grapes and plums, have a waxy coating that prevents moisture from escaping. To treat the skin, dip the fruit in boiling water for 1 minute, then pat dry with paper towel.

Other types of fruit can be sliced to a thickness of 1cm (½in).

Pre-treatment is recommended to prevent loss of vitamins and discolouration.

- Mix 1 tablespoon of lemon juice with 1 cup of water and sprinkle over the fruit as it is prepared.
- Make a sugar syrup from equal parts sugar and water. Bring to the boil, add the fruit and simmer for 1 minute. Remove the fruit with a slotted spoon, drain well, rinse carefully and pat dry with paper towel.
- Soak the fruit in fruit juice or nectar.

Depending on the type and/or thickness of the fruit, the dehydrating time will be 6–36 hours.

To reconstitute dried fruit, add 1 cup of fruit to 2 cups of water and set aside for 2 hours. The fruit can then be stewed, if desired.

Tomatoes should be cut into 1cm (½ in) slices or segments for drying. I dehydrate tomatoes to the semi-dried stage, then dip them in white vinegar before placing in a sterilised jar and covering with light olive oil. They should be stored in the fridge. If the oil tends to solidify, simply remove from the fridge shortly before serving time.

Fruit leathers

Fruit generally needs to be stewed, then pureed for fruit leathers. Very little, if any, sweetener should be used as the fruit's natural sugars concentrate as the leather dries. If you feel some sweetener is necessary, use honey as sugar has the potential to make the dried fruit leather brittle. About 2 teaspoons of honey to 2 cups of puree should be ample.

Spread the fruit puree 6mm (¼in) thick on baking paper-lined baking trays and place in the oven. Alternatively, spread the puree on special fruit leather trays and transfer to the dehydrator. The fruit leather is ready when no sticky spots are evident. To test, tear off a small piece of the leather. If no liquid is exuded, then dehydration is complete.

Remove from the trays and roll up while still warm.

VEGETABLES

Most vegetables need to be blanched before dehydrating to slow down the enzyme action that causes the vegetables to spoil. Exceptions to this are mushrooms, capsicum, onions and okra.

Most vegetables need to be sliced to a thickness of about 8mm (⅜in) for effective and consistent drying. Exceptions, of course, are peas and corn.

For best results, blanch or steam vegetables in boiling water for the same amount of time recommended for freezing (see 'Preparing vegetables for freezing' on page 63), and then plunge into iced water, drain and pat dry with paper towel.

Spread vegetables in a thin layer on baking trays and place in the oven or dehydrator, allowing room for air to circulate between the trays. Dry vegetables at a minimum of 60–70°C (140–150°F/gas ¼) for anywhere from 4–15 hours.

To test for dryness, place a piece of vegetable on a chopping board and tap with a hammer, the dried vegetable should shatter.

To reconstitute for cooking, soak each cup of dried vegetable in 2 cups of water for about 2 hours.

HERBS AND SPICES

It is important to use pesticide- and insect-free herbs that are in the very best condition. The newest leaves, that are picked in the morning, have the most flavour. Once a plant has started to flower though, the leaves have less flavour and may be bitter when dried. Flowers, such as chive flowers and rose petals, can also be dried. Again, these should be in full bloom and very fresh.

Before drying, shake the leaves or flowers to remove any insects or dirt particles, then wash and pat dry with paper towel. Herbs are not suited to oven drying, but can be dried in a food dehydrator at 35°C (95°F). Alternatively, tie herbs in bundles and hang upside down in a cool, dry place, or put in brown paper bags in a dark cupboard.

Spices, such as pepperberry, must also be fully ripe for optimum flavour after dehydrating.

MEAT

Meat should be very fresh. Remove any fat and sinew, as they will send the dried meat rancid in a very short space of time. Slice the meat with the grain into long strips about 8mm (⅜ in) thick and 2.5cm (1in) wide and marinate in an airtight plastic container in the fridge for at least 8 hours.

MARINADE FOR BEEF JERKY

This is sufficient for 1kg (2lb 4oz) of lean beef—any marinade used should contain 2 teaspoons of salt per kilogram of meat. The addition of honey in this marinade counteracts the potentially toughening effect of the salt.

¼ cup soy sauce

¼ cup tomato sauce

¼ cup white vinegar

2 teaspoons salt

1 garlic clove, crushed

1 teaspoon grated fresh green ginger

1 dessertspoon **sweet chilli sauce**

2 tablespoons honey

2 tablespoons brown sugar (optional)

Combine the ingredients in a shallow bowl and mix well. Add the meat, mix well and allow to marinate for about 6 hours in the fridge.

Preheat the oven to 70°C (150°F/gas ¼). Remove the meat from the marinade and transfer to an oven rack. Cover a baking tray with foil and place on a low shelf in the oven to catch drips from the meat. Move the meat around every now and then to prevent it from sticking to the rack as it dries.

Meat takes 6–16 hours to dry. When ready, it will be about one-quarter of its original weight. Allow to cool before testing—it will bend but not snap. Any spots of oil should be patted dry with paper towel. Store in plastic bags or airtight containers in the fridge. If the dehydrated meat is not to be used within 2 weeks, store in the freezer.

Note: *Meat can also be dried effectively in an electric food dehydrator.*

FREEZING FRUIT

Fruit should be frozen when just ripe and in prime condition, as soon as possible after picking.

PREPARING FRUIT

Work with small amounts of fruit to prevent spoilage. It is best not to add spices to fruit before freezing as the flavour of the spices is greatly diminished.

Generally, fruit frozen with a **sugar syrup** or **dry sugar** is of better quality, although this is by no means a necessity.

Note: *Fruit to be frozen and used in preserves should never have sugar added to it.*

SUGAR SYRUP

The quantity of sugar can vary according to taste and the type of fruit used.

    250g (9oz) sugar
    2 cups water

Combine the sugar and water in a saucepan over medium heat and bring to the boil, stirring until the sugar has dissolved. Allow to cool before use. For each 1kg (2lb 4oz) of fruit, use about 1 cup of cold sugar syrup.

Dry sugar

The amount of dry sugar recommended for freezing fruit is 250g (9oz) for each 1kg (2lb 4oz)) of fruit. Carefully mix the sugar through the fruit before packaging for the freezer.

Some fruit, such as apples, apricots, peaches and nectarines, discolour during preparation and/or freezing. To help prevent this, try one of the methods below.

Ascorbic acid powder

Add this powder (obtained from good home-brewing shops) to the fresh fruit, fruit puree or sugar syrup.

For fresh fruit, mix ¼ teaspoon of ascorbic acid powder with ¼ cup cold water and stir to dissolve. This amount can be mixed into 1kg (2lb 4oz) of fruit before placing in airtight containers or bags and freezing.

If using a sugar syrup to cover fruit for freezing, then add ½ teaspoon of ascorbic acid powder to each 1 litre (35fl oz) of sugar syrup used.

Citric acid or lemon juice

Mix 1½ teaspoons of citric acid or 3 tablespoons of lemon juice into each 1 litre (35fl oz) of water. Dip the fruit into the solution, drain well and pat dry with paper towel before freezing.

Steam blanching

To steam blanch, place the fruit in a steamer basket over a saucepan of boiling water. Cover with a lid and steam for 3 minutes.

Preparing fruit for freezing

Fruit	Preparation
Apples	Peel, core and slice. Scald in boiling water, then plunge into iced water. Drain and pat dry, then pack with dry sugar or sugar syrup
Apricots	Peel if desired by dipping in boiling water for 20 seconds, then plunge briefly into iced water. Halve and remove stones. Use dry sugar or sugar syrup with ascorbic acid, citric acid or lemon juice
Bananas	Freeze whole with or without skins or mash and add 1 tablespoon of lemon juice for each cup of puree
Berry fruits	Tray freeze individually before packaging or use dry sugar or sugar syrup
Citrus fruits	Wash, peel and segment. Sprinkle with dry sugar to taste and allow to stand for 2 hours. Pack into containers and freeze
Cherries: sour and sweet	Freeze whole or pitted. Tray freeze in a single layer, then place in containers. Alternatively, pack in sugar syrup with ascorbic acid or lemon juice added

Fruit	Preparation
Cranberries	Tray freeze in a single layer, then pack in freezer containers. Do not add sugar
Currants (red, black and white)	Remove stems, wash in cold water. Drain well. Freeze in a single layer on trays before packaging
Feijoas	Peel, wash and remove pips. Freeze whole, halved or pureed. Add ascorbic acid powder, citric acid or lemon juice to prevent discolouration
Figs	Try to freeze no more than 12 hours after picking. Remove stems, peel and slice. Freeze in sugar syrup with ascorbic acid added
Grapes	Wash and dry. Freeze in a single layer on trays before packaging. Do not add dry sugar. Use sugar syrup, if desired
Guavas	Texture changes with freezing. Wash, peel, halve and remove seeds. Freeze halves or puree. Best preserved in sugar syrup
Kiwi fruit	Peel and freeze whole, cut into slices or puree. For slices, freeze in a single layer on trays before packaging
Loquats	Wash, remove stems, blossom ends and seeds. Cover with sugar syrup and freeze
Lychees	Wash and freeze with skin on. Alternatively, peel, cut in half, remove pip and freeze in containers in sugar syrup
Mangoes	Use just-ripe fruit. Peel and remove stone, cut into slices and freeze in sugar syrup. Alternatively, puree the mango flesh and freeze
Melons	Peel, remove seeds and cut into cubes or balls. Freeze in sugar syrup

Fruit	Preparation
Peaches/ nectarines	Dip in boiling water for 20 seconds then plunge briefly into iced water to remove skins. Peel, remove stones, slice and pack in sugar syrup with ascorbic acid added
Pears	Wash, peel and core. Slice into 8 sections. Dip in boiling sugar syrup. Drain, cool and pack in sugar syrup with ascorbic acid added
Persimmons	Freeze whole or make a puree (add $1/4$ teaspoon ascorbic acid or 3 teaspoons citric acid per 2 litres (70fl oz) of puree)
Pineapples	Peel and core, dice, slice or cut into chunks. Pack in sugar syrup or dry sugar
Plums	Wash. Leave whole or halve and remove stones. Pack in dry sugar or sugar syrup with lemon juice, citric acid or ascorbic acid added
Pomegranates	Halve and push out seeds. Freeze in small containers
Quinces	Peel, quarter, steam or blanch for 3 minutes, plunge briefly into iced water, and tray freeze before packaging
Rhubarb	Choose well-coloured red stalks. Remove leaves and tough stalks. Cut stalks into 2.5cm (1in) pieces. Do not blanch. Pack with or without dry sugar

Hint: *For future jelly making, cook the fruit and strain off the juice using the jelly making procedure, then freeze the juice in containers. The fruit jelly can later be prepared by thawing this juice, adding sugar and boiling until setting point is reached.*

PACKAGING FRUIT

Fruit can be frozen in freezer bags or containers. For freezer bags, place the fruit in the bag, allowing 1.5cm (⅝ in) headspace, and insert a plastic drinking straw into the space around the fruit. Squeeze the neck of the bag in around the straw and suck out the air, remembering to allow for headspace (this is necessary as the fruit expands as it freezes). Remove the straw, pinching in the top of the bag and fasten immediately with the bag tie. For containers, fill with fruit to within 1.5cm (⅝ in) of the top, then cover with the lid.

For free-flowing product, fruit (whole, sliced or diced) can also be tray frozen. The prepared fruit is placed on a tray in a single layer, sprinkled with sugar (optional) and frozen. Pack into bags or containers as soon as it is frozen (extended exposure results in loss of moisture). It is not necessary to leave headspace.

Place the bags or containers in the coldest part of the freezer. Allow 2.5cm (1 in) around each package for faster freezing. Once the food is frozen, the packages can then be placed tightly together.

Frozen fruit will keep, stored at -18°C (0°F) or lower, for 8–12 months. It is highly advisable to buy a fridge/freezer thermometer so that this can be monitored—the cost is minimal.

Note: *Freezer burn is caused by exposure to air. It affects the texture of the fruit and to some extent the flavour. The fruit isn't unsafe to eat, but it may be dry, leathery and discoloured. Cut out these portions before using. To avoid freezer burn, ensure that all air is removed from the packaging before freezing.*

FREEZING VEGETABLES

Use only very fresh vegetables in prime condition: never over-ripe or under-ripe. It is best to work with small quantities at a time.

PREPARING VEGETABLES

It is necessary to blanch most vegetables before freezing.

To blanch the vegetables, bring 5 litres (175fl oz) of water to a rolling boil in a saucepan. Place up to 500g (1lb 2oz) of prepared vegetables in a single layer in a wire basket, immerse in the water and cover with the lid. Begin counting blanching time when steam escapes from under the lid.

Vegetables may also be steam-blanched. Bring 3 cups of water to the boil in a saucepan. Place the prepared vegetables in a steamer basket above the water and cover with the lid. Steam blanching takes longer than the boiling water method and is not suited to all types of vegetables.

Basil is the only herb that needs to be blanched. Blanch the leaves for 30 seconds only.

After blanching, plunge the vegetables into ice-cold water, drain thoroughly and pat dry with paper towel. Cool thoroughly before packaging for freezing.

Preparing vegetables for freezing

Vegetable	Preparation	Water blanching time
Asparagus	Wash, leave whole or cut into short lengths	2–3 minutes, depending on size
Beans	Wash, trim, leave whole or cut into lengths	3 minutes
Broad beans	Shell and wash	3 minutes
Broccoli	Wash, cut into florets	3 minutes
Brussels sprouts	Wash, remove outer leaves	2–4 minutes, depending on size
Cabbage	Cut off outer leaves. Wash, cut into wedges or shred coarsely	Wedges—3 minutes Shredded—1 $\frac{1}{2}$ minutes
Capsicums	Wash, dry, remove stems, seeds and membranes. Freeze halves or cut into slice or dice	Not required
Carrots	Wash, leave small carrots whole, cut larger ones into 8mm ($\frac{3}{8}$ in) thick slices	2 minutes

Vegetable	Preparation	Water blanching Time
Cauliflower	Remove outer leaves, wash, cut into florets	3 minutes
Corn on the cob	Remove husks and silks, trim off ends	5–7 minutes, depending on size
Corn kernels	Blanch whole cobs, chill in iced water, cut corn from cob	As above
Creamed corn	As for whole kernels, plus scrape cobs with the back of a knife to obtain juice	As above
Eggplant	Wash, trim ends, peel, cut into 1cm ($\frac{1}{2}$in) slices. Add $\frac{1}{2}$ cup lemon juice to blanching water	4 minutes
Kohlrabi	Wash, remove tops, cut into 8mm ($\frac{3}{8}$in) slices or dice, wash again	2 minutes
Mushrooms	Wash, remove stems, pat dry. Use small mushrooms whole. Slice larger mushrooms	Steam blanch for 3–4 minutes
	or	
	Sauté in a little butter or oil and cool before freezing, if desired	Not necessary
Onions	Peel and chop, wrap in small quantities in cling wrap, place in freezer bags or containers	Not necessary

Vegetable	Preparation	Water blanching Time
Parsnips	Wash and peel. Use whole, sliced or diced	Whole—5 minutes Sliced or diced—$2\frac{1}{2}$ minutes
Peas	Wash, shell	$1\frac{1}{2}$ minutes
Potatoes	Wash, peel, wash again. Cut into 2.5cm (1in) slices or 1.25cm ($\frac{1}{2}$in) dice	4 minutes
New potatoes	Wash, scrub, wash again	Small—4 minutes Larger—5–8 minutes, depending on size
Potatoes for chips or French fries	Cut peeled potatoes into strips, deep fry until lightly brown. Drain and cool	Not applicable
Pumpkin	Cook pumpkin as usual, drain, mash, cool	Not applicable
Spinach and silverbeet	Remove stems, wash, dry, shred	2 minutes
Tomatoes	Wash, remove stalks, cook until soft	Not applicable
Zucchini	Wash, trim ends, cut into batons or strips	3 minutes

PACKAGING VEGETABLES

There are two ways to package vegetables for freezing.

Method I

Pack the drained and dried vegetables into portion-sized freezer bags, allowing 1cm (½in) headspace. Make sure that as little air as possible remains in the bag by inserting a plastic drinking straw into the space around the vegetables. Squeeze the neck of the bag in around the straw and suck out the air, remembering to allow for headspace (this is necessary as vegetables expand as they freeze). Pinch the neck of the bag tight as the straw is removed and secure immediately with the bag tie.

The prepared vegetables can also be packed into freezer containers and sealed, leaving 1cm (½in) headspace in container to allow for expansion during freezing.

No more than 10 per cent of the freezer should be used for the packed vegetables. This is because the temperature of the freezer can be altered by the addition of the unfrozen products which may contribute to spoilage of the original contents of the freezer. Allow 1cm (½in) of space around each freezer bag or container until the vegetables are completely frozen, then pack together tightly.

The temperature in the freezer should be a steady -17°C (0°F) or lower. I recommend buying a fridge/freezer thermometer so that this can be monitored. Vegetables stored in these conditions can be frozen for up to 12 months.

Method 2

For free-flowing vegetables, spread the blanched and dried vegetables in a single layer on a tray and freeze. Pack into bags or containers as soon as they are frozen. There is no need to leave any headspace as vegetables are already frozen.

Note: *Freezer burn is caused by exposure to air. It affects the texture of the vegetables and to some extent the flavour. The vegetable isn't unsafe to eat, but it may be dry, leathery and discoloured. Cut out these portions before using. To avoid freezer burn, ensure that as much air as possible is removed from the packaging before freezing.*

COOKING FROZEN VEGETABLES

Steam or cook in a small amount of boiling water for about half the amount of time it takes to cook from fresh.

EASY
ESSENTIAL
RECIPES

BASIC BREAD DOUGH

For many years, even before I was married, I battled with bread dough. Results ranged from fair to disastrous. A turning point came when a Swedish friend showed me how she made her exceptional bread, a method she had learned in a cooking school in her home country. She told me that it is important not to make the dough too tight. By adding more liquid and thus making a softer dough, you allow the yeast to do its work more easily. After that, making bread products became a passion.

Baking bread is one of the most satisfying things you can do in the kitchen, right alongside preserving. Again, you have control over what goes into the end product.

Children love kneading dough. When our children were little, as well as playdough, I would give them bread dough to knead and play with. It taught them the nature of bread dough—how it feels and behaves under different conditions and the effects of adding other ingredients—and they could cook it and eat it later.

Kneading bread is very therapeutic and bread dough is very forgiving. The more you knead and bash it, the better it likes it— wonderful for anyone in an ill humour, child and adult alike.

The following is a formula I developed for a light bread dough. It is designed to be multiplied according to the quantity you need. For example, for a large loaf that serves 4–6 people, use 3–4 cups of plain flour, with the other ingredients multiplied accordingly.

> 1 cup plain flour (you can use half wholemeal and
>   half plain)
> ¾ teaspoon sugar
> ½ teaspoon salt
> 1 teaspoon dried yeast
> 2 teaspoons oil, such as light olive oil, canola or peanut oil
> warm water (see Note)

Combine the flour, sugar, salt and yeast in a large bowl. Make a well in the centre and add the oil together with enough warm water to make a soft scone dough. Mix well, cover with a clean tea towel and set aside in a warm place for about 1 hour, or until doubled in size.

Turn the dough over with a metal spoon, and allow to rise again. This will take about 30 minutes. Repeat this process several times if you want, or just once will do if you are short on time.

Turn the dough out onto a lightly floured surface and knead until smooth. If it has been through the rising process a couple of times, 3 minutes is sufficient. Shape into a loaf, bread rolls or pizza bases. If making a loaf of bread, half fill the loaf tin with the dough. Allow dough to rise almost to the top of the tin. If making rolls or pizza bases, transfer the shaped dough to greased baking trays. Allow rolls to rise for 15 minutes. If adding toppings to pizza base, leave to stand for 5 minutes before baking.

Preheat the oven to 200°C (400°F/gas 6). Bake for:

❖ 10 minutes at 200°C (400°F/gas 6) for a larger loaf, then at 170°C (325°F/gas 3) for a further 20–25 minutes. The bread is cooked if it makes a hollow sound when the top is tapped with the fingers;

❖ 12–15 minutes for bread rolls;

❖ 15–20 minutes for pizza base with toppings.

Note: *As flours and humidity levels vary, it isn't possible to give a definitive amount of water required as this can change from day to day. Just remember the principle of making a soft but manageable dough.*

CHOCOLATE CAKE

125g (4½oz/½ cup) butter
1½ cups sugar
¼ cup cocoa powder
½ teaspoon bicarbonate of soda
1 cup water
2 eggs
1¼ cups self-raising flour
¼ cup plain flour
½ teaspoon baking powder
1 dessertspoon custard powder
½ teaspoon vanilla extract

Place the butter, sugar, cocoa, bicarbonate of soda and water in a large saucepan over medium heat and bring to the boil. Immediately reduce heat to low and simmer for 3 minutes. Remove from the heat and set aside to cool for 15 minutes.

Meanwhile, preheat the oven to 170°C (325°F/gas 3). Grease a 20cm (8in) deep-sided round cake tin and line the base with baking paper.

Quickly whisk the eggs into the chocolate mixture, then add flours, baking powder and custard powder and whisk until smooth. Stir in the vanilla extract. Pour into the greased tin. Bake for 30 minutes, or until a metal skewer inserted into the centre of the cake comes out clean. Leave to stand in the tin for 5 minutes, then turn out onto a cake cooler. To serve, cut the cake into slices and drizzle with **ganache**.

Serves 8

CRÈME CHANTILLY

300ml (10½fl oz) thickened cream
2 teaspoons icing sugar
¼ teaspoon vanilla extract
pinch of powdered gelatine

Whip the cream, icing sugar and vanilla in a large bowl until soft peaks form. Add the gelatine and whip to firm peaks.

Makes approximately 1½ cups

GANACHE

2 cups pouring or thickened cream
500g (1lb 2 oz) dark cooking chocolate, cut into small pieces

Place the cream in a saucepan and bring to the boil. Remove from the heat, add the chocolate and stir until smooth. Allow to cool to a spreading consistency, or serve immediately as a sauce.

Use this ganache to glaze chocolate cakes. If the ganache is cooled to room temperature until it starts to thicken, it can be whipped to make a fudgy chocolate icing or it can be piped as decorations.

The ganache will keep in an airtight container in the fridge for 1–2 weeks. To soften, reheat in the microwave on MEDIUM in 20-second bursts, or spoon into a small saucepan and melt over low heat on the stovetop.

Makes approximately 4 cups

CURRIED BREADCRUMBS

90g (3¼oz/⅓ cup) butter
2 teaspoons curry powder
2 cups fresh breadcrumbs, approximately

Melt the butter in a small saucepan, add the curry powder and gently fry for 1 minute, or until aromatic. Add enough breadcrumbs to absorb the butter mixture. Cook until the crumbs are well coated with the butter and beginning to crisp.

Use as a topping for chilli pumpkin tartlets, or in place of pastry for mustardy chicken pie or crayfish pot pies.

Makes about 2 cups

Hint: *Make up a double batch of this mixture and keep it in a jar in the fridge ready to use as a quick topping for a variety of savoury dishes.*

PANCAKES

125g (4½oz) plain flour
½ teaspoon salt
1 egg
250–300ml (9–10½fl oz) water or milk

Combine the flour and salt in a bowl. Make a well in the centre and all at once, add the egg and enough water or milk to make a thin batter. Whisk until smooth, then set aside to stand for 30 minutes, if possible.

Spray a frying pan with cooking oil or lightly grease with butter, and place over medium heat. Pour about 2 tablespoons of the batter into the pan and spread thinly over the base. Cook until the underside is just golden, then turn with a spatula or egg flip to briefly cook on the other. Do not allow the pancakes to brown.

Makes approximately 8 pancakes

Hints: *Pancakes have a range of sweet and savoury applications. They can also be made with gluten-free plain flour and can be used in place of lasagne noodles.*

Left-over pancakes can be made into the simplest dessert, a favourite with children. Simply drizzle each warm pancake with a little lemon juice, sprinkle on a little sugar and roll up. Totally delicious!

SHORTCRUST PASTRY

This shortcrust pastry is great for tasty and delectable meat pie, spooner pie, chilli pumpkin tartlets, chilli chicken parcels, green eggs and ham pie, mini mustard quiches, mustardy chicken pie, beef and mushroom pie, beef and mushroom pot pies and crayfish pot pies.

180g (6¼oz) plain flour
1½ teaspoons baking powder
½ teaspoon salt
90g (3¼oz) butter, diced
1 egg yolk, lightly whisked
2 teaspoons lemon juice
½ cup cold water, approximately

Combine the flour, baking powder and salt in a mixing bowl and rub in the butter with your fingertips until the mixture resembles breadcrumbs, or process to this stage in a food processor, then transfer to a mixing bowl. Add the egg yolk, lemon juice and half the water and stir with a metal spoon until the dough comes together to form a soft dough. If the mixture is too dry, add a little more water. Wrap in cling film and place in the fridge for 30 minutes. (This makes the pastry easier to roll.)

Roll out the dough on a lightly floured surface until 5mm (¼in) thick.

Makes approximately 350g (12oz)

Hint: *Any left-over dough can be wrapped in cling film and placed in the fridge. Use within a few days.*

SWEET SHORTCRUST PASTRY

This pastry could be used for apple and coconut tart, felties and Nanna's little cheesecakes.

> 125g (4½oz) butter, softened
> 125g (4½oz) sugar
> 1 egg
> 30g (1oz) custard powder
> 95g (3¼oz) plain flour
> 125g (4½oz) self-raising flour

Cream the butter and sugar in a bowl, then whisk in the egg until well combined. Add the custard powder and the combined flours and stir until the dough is well mixed. Wrap in cling film and place in the fridge for at least 30 minutes before using.

Makes 2 x 20cm (8in) tarts

VARIATIONS

Left-over pastry can be used to make plain sweet biscuits that can be joined with raspberry or strawberry jam and iced to make kiss biscuits.

For fruit pies, try adding 1½ teaspoons finely grated lemon or lime zest when creaming the butter and sugar.

USING
HOMEMADE
PRESERVES

APPLES

As a child, we often visited the orchards of my uncles and great grandparents in the renowned apple growing region of the Huon Valley. I still remember the lengthy winding trip through the foothills of Mount Wellington and emerging into the valley with its seemingly endless and perfectly symmetrical rows of apple trees. I clearly recall apple blossom time; the scent of apples hanging heavy in the late spring air. And in the autumn, roadside stalls piled high with apples, the country fairs with delicious, crunchy toffee apples and apple pies and tarts proudly baked by the local ladies. Each year a prestigious event was held where a young lady of the region was bestowed with the title of Apple Queen for the year.

My uncles during these autumn visits would take us with our cousins to the packing sheds, supposing we should like to try our hand at packing and sorting. As children of course we showed little interest, I suspect much to the relief of the cheery rosy-cheeked apple packers, who sent us on our way with an armload to enjoy as we played in the orchards.

Fifty years later, we still travel to the Huon each year in search of the best cooking apples, such as Granny Smiths and Sturmers, and if at all possible Bramleys, to stock the pantry shelves and freezer so that we can produce tasty pies and tarts during the coming months.

APPLE PULP

—⊃

Always try to use cooking apples such as Granny Smiths, Sturmers or Bramleys, as they produce a really smooth pulp. That being said, I do sometimes use a combination of cooking and eating apples. In this way you obtain a smooth pulp, but with small pieces of cooked but still firm apple flesh in the mixture, as a result of the eating apples being included.

Making apple pulp is a simple process.

> 1kg (2lb 4oz) apples, peeled, cored and chopped
> ½ cup water

Peel and core the apples and cut the flesh into 1cm (½in) slices. Place the apple in a large saucepan, add the water and cook over low–medium heat, stirring often, for about 20 minutes, or until reduced and pulpy.

Makes approximately 1kg (2lb 4oz)

PRESERVING APPLE PULP

Apple pulp can be preserved in jars using the classic water-bath method. However, because it is generally quite dense, I find I usually end up smearing the pulp all around the rim of the preserving jar, where it tends to stick like glue and may affect the sealing process. To avoid this, freeze the cooled apple pulp in inexpensive, re-usable rectangular food containers that will hold enough for a crumble, pie or tart. Take the container out of the freezer the night before it is needed. If you forget, it's easy to defrost the pulp in the microwave in just a few minutes.

APPLE AND COCONUT TART

1 sheet frozen puff pastry, thawed
375g (13oz) frozen **apple pulp**, thawed
¼–½ cup sugar
4 teaspoons custard powder mixed to a smooth paste with
   about ¼ cup cold water

TOPPING
60g (2¼oz/¼ cup) butter, softened
125g (4½oz) sugar
1 egg
60g (2¼oz) desiccated coconut

Line a 20cm (8in) pie dish with the pastry, trimming the edge of the dish of excess pastry. Place in the fridge until required.

For the filling, place the apple pulp in a saucepan over medium heat and bring to the boil. Add sugar to taste and stir in the custard powder paste. Continue to stir until the apple mixture has thickened slightly. Set aside to cool.

Preheat the oven to 200°C (400°F/gas 6).

For the topping, whisk the butter and sugar together. Whisk in the egg and then stir in the coconut with a metal spoon. The topping should be a soft consistency. Set aside.

Pour the filling into the pastry case and smooth the surface with the back of a spoon. Place blobs of the topping evenly over the filling and spread out with a spatula or knife, making sure that the filling is completely covered.

Bake for 10 minutes. Reduce the oven temperature to 150°C (300°F/gas 2) and bake for a further 20 minutes, or until the topping is golden and set. Serve with ice cream, cream or plain yoghurt.

Serves 6

APPLE TARTLETS

a little egg white, for brushing
1 x quantity **sweet shortcrust pastry**
approximately 250g (9oz) **apple pulp**
sugar, to taste
1 tablespoon icing sugar, for dusting
1 teaspoon ground cinnamon

Preheat the oven to 180°C (350°F/gas 4). Grease 24 (¼-cup capacity) scoop patty pan holes.

Roll out the pastry on a lightly floured surface to 3mm (⅛in) thick. Cut out 24 rounds to fit the patty pan holes. Press into the pans and brush with a little egg white right to the edge of the pasty. Cut out 24 smaller rounds to form lids for the tartlets, re-rolling scraps of pastry if necessary.

Sweeten the apple pulp to taste with a little sugar. Place 2 teaspoons of the apple pulp in each pastry case. Place the pastry lids on top and press the edges together. Prick each tartlet once with a fork. Bake for 12–15 minutes or until lightly browned. Allow to stand in the pans for 5 minutes, then transfer to a wire rack to cool completely. To serve, dust with icing sugar and cinnamon.

Makes approximately 24

APPLE CUSTARD SHORTCAKE

375g (13oz) **apple pulp**

sugar, to taste

5 teaspoons custard powder mixed to a smooth paste with
   about ⅓ cup cold water

125g (4½oz) butter, softened

125g (4½oz) sugar

1 egg

125g (4½oz) self-raising flour, sifted

125g (4½oz) plain flour, sifted

a little egg white, for brushing

1 cup sultanas

finely grated zest of 1 lemon

Place the apple pulp in a saucepan over medium heat and bring to the boil.
Sweeten to taste with the sugar, stir in the custard powder paste and cook
until thickened, stirring constantly. Set aside to cool. If you want to hasten the
cooling process, spread the apple mixture onto a cold plate.

Cream the butter and sugar. Add the egg and whisk until well combined.
Add the flours and fold in with a metal spoon to form a soft dough. Wrap the
dough in cling film and put in the fridge for at least 30 minutes.

Preheat the oven to 170°C (325°F/gas 3). Grease an 18 x 28cm
(7 x 11¼ in) slab tin.

Divide the chilled dough in half. Roll out each portion on a lightly floured
surface to form a rectangle the size of the tin. Place one portion in the tin
and brush with the egg white.

Sprinkle the sultanas over the pastry, then sprinkle on the lemon zest. Spread the cooled apple mixture on top and cover with the remaining pastry. Prick several times with a fork and bake for 30 minutes or until golden brown. Allow to cool a little in the tin, then cut into squares and serve with **crème chantilly**, custard or ice cream.

Serve immediately as a dessert, or allow to cool and dust with icing sugar or ice with lemon icing (see page 98).

Serves 8

Roast Pork with Spiced Apple Sauce

——◦

2 tablespoons canola or peanut oil

1.5kg (3lb 5oz) boned leg or loin of pork

3 teaspoons salt

1 tablespoon white or cider vinegar

½ cup chicken or vegetable stock

Jus

¼ cup dry white wine

2 teaspoons tomato paste

1 teaspoon **quince jelly**

1½ cups chicken or vegetable stock, extra

3 teaspoons cornflour mixed to a smooth paste with about
    2 tablespoons of cold water

salt and pepper

Spiced apple sauce

1 cup **apple pulp**

2 teaspoons sugar

½ teaspoon allspice

½ teaspoon ground cloves

¼ teaspoon ground cinnamon

Preheat the oven to 220°C (425°F/gas 7).

Pour the oil into a roasting tin and place in the oven for five minutes to heat.

Meanwhile, slash the pork rind at 1.5cm (⅝in) intervals with a sharp knife. Rub with the vinegar, then with the salt.

Place the pork in the roasting tin and pour the ½ cup of stock around the base of the meat. Roast for 15 minutes, then reduce the oven temperature to 170°C (325°F/gas 3) and roast for a further 1½ hours, or until juices run clear when the centre of the roast is pierced with a carving fork. Transfer the pork to a plate, cover loosely with foil and make several slashes in the top to ensure the crackling remains crisp. Set aside to rest in a warm place.

For the jus, pour excess fat from the roasting tin, leaving about ⅓ cup of pan juices. Place the roasting tin over medium heat. Pour in the wine and stir to deglaze the pan. Add the tomato paste, quince jelly and extra stock. Bring to the boil and simmer for 2 minutes. Strain, if desired. Thicken with enough of the cornflour paste to make a thin gravy-like consistency. Add salt and pepper to taste.

For the spiced apple sauce, heat the apple pulp in a small saucepan over medium heat, sweeten with the sugar and mix in the spices.

Serve slices of the pork with the jus and a spoonful of the spiced apple sauce. Accompany with roast potato, pumpkin and parsnip.

Serves 6

APRICOTS

We have a friend, Pene, who is extremely generous with the fruit from her garden. It is an average suburban garden that is organically cultivated with fruit contentedly growing in wild profusion.

Each year she calls to offer me her excess summer fruit. For instance, last summer when we were driving to Hobart, Pene let me know that the apricots were ripe for the picking, as was a large crop of boysenberries. Too far from home to return for buckets, we bought some from a nearby supermarket and arrived on her doorstep within the hour. The apricots were, as always, sensational. The tree was absolutely laden and so obliging that merely touching the fruit will drop it into your waiting hand, perfect, bursting with flavour and colour—tender enough to eat, yet firm enough to bottle to perfection.

Picking the boysenberries is a risky business. They have lethal thorns, nasty little fine things that grab at your clothes and fingers—the price you pay, Pene says, for their most delicious deep purple berries that make sensational jams, cordials and pies.

We grew them once ourselves when we lived in suburbia. Our old beagle hound, Henry, absolutely loved them. Many were the times that the children went to pick a bowl of berries for dinner and there were none to be found on the bushes. Henry's purple stained nose revealed the identity of the culprit.

APRICOT PULP

—⊃

Making apricot pulp is a simple process.

> 1kg (2lb 4oz) apricots, peeled, cored and chopped
> ½ cup water

Peel and remove the stones from the apricots. Cut the flesh into 1cm (½in) slices. Grease a large saucepan with butter. This helps prevent the apricots from burning. Put the apricots in the saucepan and add the water. Cook over low–medium heat, stirring frequently, for about 20 minutes, or until reduced and pulpy.

Makes approximately 1kg (2lb 4oz)

FREEZING APRICOT PULP

Freeze the cooled apricot pulp in inexpensive, reusable rectangular food containers that will hold enough for a crumble, pie or tart. Take the container out of the freezer the night before it is needed. If you forget, it's easy to defrost the pulp in the microwave in just a few minutes.

BOTTLED APRICOT HALVES

Apricot halves are simplicity itself to bottle and look sensational on the pantry shelves. To my mind, they are one of the most versatile of all preserved products.

> 2kg (4lb 8oz) apricots, washed, halved and stones removed
> preserving syrup of choice (see opposite)

Place the sealing rings on clean preserving jars.

Layer the apricots, skin side up, neatly and firmly in the bottles. Pour the preserving liquid over the apricots right to the brim. Place the lids on the bottles and secure with the clips, or if using screw-top jars, screw the lids on.

Place the jars in the preserving outfit. Fill preserver with cool water to just cover the lids. Bring to 95°C (203°F), making sure that this takes at least 1 hour. Hold at this temperature for 30 minutes for bottles containing up to 10 cups of product, add an extra 15 minutes for larger jars.

Remove the jars from the preserver and place on a chopping board. Leave to stand for 24 hours. Remove the clips, if using, and check that the lids are concave.

Store in a cool, dark and dry place for 12 months. (Actually, I don't for the most part—I like to leave the bottles out where I can admire their colour on the pantry shelves. It doesn't really seem to do them any harm. Maybe after a few months they start to lose their bright colour a little, but then I just use them and replace with other jars from the darker recesses of the cupboard.)

Makes 4–5 x 500g (1lb 2oz) jars

PRESERVING SYRUP

The preserving liquid can be water, fruit juice or sugar syrup. The sugar syrup used will vary according to taste:

light syrup: one part sugar to four parts water
medium syrup: one part sugar to two parts water
heavy syrup: equal parts sugar and water

I make the sugar syrup in a plastic jug. For instance, to make a heavy syrup, half fill the jug with sugar, add enough boiling water to dissolve, then fill the remainder of the jug with cold water. Cool. The syrup is then ready to use. Any left-over syrup can be stored in the fridge for 3 days (light syrup) and 7 days (heavy syrup).

APRICOT CHICKEN PARCELS

This recipe has been a favourite for years. I prefer the parcels made with filo pastry; my children's preference is for puff pastry. Often I make a double batch as they are very tasty the next day as a chilled lunch box treat.

2 large chicken breast fillets, cut in half

3 tablespoons plain flour

60g (2¼oz/¼ cup) butter

1 tablespoon olive oil, plus extra

800g (1lb 12oz) **bottled apricot halves**, drained and juice
   reserved

4 tablespoons finely chopped mint

½ teaspoon salt (optional)

8 sheets filo pastry

¼ cup milk

Preheat the oven to 180°C (350°F/gas 4). Grease a baking tray.

Dust the chicken in the flour, seasoned with a little salt and pepper.

Heat the butter and oil in a large frying pan over medium–high heat. Add the chicken and brown on all sides. Transfer the chicken onto crumpled paper towel to drain. Set aside to cool.

Meanwhile, add the apricot halves to the pan and stir to coat with the pan juices. Add the mint and immediately remove from the heat. Set aside to cool.

Place one sheet of filo pastry on a lightly floured bench, brush with a little extra oil, top with another sheet of pastry. Place 1 tablespoon of minted apricot halves in the centre of the pastry and top with a chicken portion. Lightly dampen the edges of the pastry with a little water and fold up to enclose the filling, making a parcel. Transfer to the greased tray. Repeat to make another three parcels.

Brush the top of each filo parcel with a little milk. Bake for 30 minutes or until golden brown.

Add the reserved juice from the apricots to the remaining minted apricot mixture in the pan. Bring to the boil over medium heat and cook, stirring, until the sauce has reduced and thickened a little. If the apricots do not break down as they cook, mash them with a fork or puree the mixture.

To serve, spoon some apricot sauce onto each plate and place an apricot chicken parcel on top.

Serves 4

VARIATION
You may like to cut a pocket in each chicken portion and insert a small slice of camembert before wrapping in the pastry.

Apricot Crumble

800g (1lb 12oz) **bottled apricots halves**, drained retaining
   ½ cup juice
sugar, to taste
1 cup self-raising flour
⅔ cup brown sugar, firmly packed
60g (2¼oz/¼ cup) butter, cubed

Preheat the oven to 170°C (325°F/gas 3).

Place the apricot halves and the reserved juice in a casserole dish. Taste the apricots and sweeten, if necessary, by sprinkling the sugar over the top and mixing through.

Combine the flour and brown sugar in a bowl. Rub in the butter with your fingertips until the mixture resembles breadcrumbs. Alternatively, place the flour, brown sugar and butter in the bowl of a food processor and process until well combined.

Sprinkle the crumble evenly over the top of the apricots. Bake for 30 minutes, or until crumble topping is golden brown.

Serve with ice cream, yoghurt or whipped cream.

Serves 6

VARIATION

Frozen cooked **apricot pulp**, sweetened to taste, could be substituted for the bottled apricot halves in this recipe.

Microwave Apricot Sponge Pudding

400g (14oz) **bottled apricot halves** or **apricot pulp**
½ cup sugar (optional)
60g (2¼oz/¼ cup) butter, softened
½ cup sugar, extra
1 egg
1 cup self-raising flour
½ cup milk
2 tablespoons lemon juice
1 teaspoon ground cinnamon
1 tablespoon caster sugar
icing sugar, for dusting

Grease a 23cm (9in) deep-sided, round, microwave-safe casserole dish.

Heat the apricots in a saucepan over medium heat, stirring constantly. If you wish, sweeten to taste with ½ cup sugar. Spoon into the greased dish.

Cream the butter and ½ cup sugar with a wooden spoon or metal whisk until light and fluffy. Add the egg and whisk until well combined. Fold in the flour, milk and lemon juice all at once. Pour the sponge mixture evenly over the hot fruit.

Cook in the microwave on HIGH for 12 minutes, or until an area the size of a 10-cent coin in the centre of the topping is just slightly sticky. If the topping is sticky over a greater area, return to the microwave and cook for 1 minute more. Remove from the microwave and dust with icing sugar before serving.

Serves 6

Hint: *Any type of bottled or stewed fruit can be used in this recipe. If the fruit mixture is too liquid, thicken with a cornflour paste made from mixing 1 tablespoon of cornflour with ¼ cup of cold water.*

APRICOT TEA CAKE

½ cup milk

2 tablespoons lemon or lime juice

1 egg

¾ cup sugar

1½ cups self-raising flour

60g (2¼ oz) butter, melted

grated zest of 1 lemon or lime (optional)

12 **bottled apricot halves**, drained

1½ teaspoons ground cinnamon

2 tablespoons caster sugar

2 tablespoons butter, melted

Preheat the oven to 170°C (325°F/gas 3). Grease and line the base of 20cm (8in) round cake tin.

Combine the milk and lemon or lime juice in a jug and set aside.

Whisk the egg and sugar in a medium bowl until pale and thick. Add the combined milk and juice, the flour and melted butter all at once and whisk until smooth. Stir in the lemon or lime zest, if using. Pour the mixture into the prepared tin. Top with the apricot halves and bake for 30 minutes, or until a skewer inserted into the centre of the cake comes out clean. Allow the cake to stand in the tin for a few minutes, and then transfer onto a cake cooler and turn right way up.

For the topping, combine the cinnamon and sugar in a small bowl. Brush the top of the cake while still hot with the melted butter, then sprinkle with the cinnamon sugar. This cake is delicious served warm or cold.

Serves 6–8

VARIATION

Preserved peach or nectarine halves or stoned plums can be substituted for apricots.

Note: *If this cake is to be stored for more than 1 day, allow to cool completely, then put in an airtight container and place in the fridge.*

Dehydrating pre-preserved apricots

Our youngest daughter, Courtney, is a great experimenter with dehydrating food. She began with herbs from her extensive herb garden and then moved on to target my bottled preserves. Not that it mattered, mind you; I have shelves bulging with preserves, and I'm always short on jars.

One day, while watching me despair because I didn't have enough jars for the latest arrival of fruit, she decided to try converting last year's bottles of apricot halves into dried apricots.

We were both astounded at how well they turned out. No pre-treatment was necessary: the apricots retained their lovely bright colour and were a taste sensation. Children love them, of course, and they are a far better alternative to lollies.

I had bottled a particular variety of apricot that was not at all satisfactory. They were a soggy, sloppy mess when turned out of the bottle. Courtney drained these, mashed them to remove any lumps and made fruit leather sheets out of them. These apricots had also been particularly bitter, almost unpalatable, in fact. The dehydrating process concentrated the natural sugars, and so the end result was most pleasing. They still retained a little tang, but were certainly sweet enough to eat.

DRIED APRICOTS

———○

Courtney, a classic non-breakfast eater, used to take these to school with her and eat them during the day.

800g (1lb 12oz) **bottled apricot halves**

Drain the apricot halves and pat dry with paper towel. Place the apricots on the racks of the dehydrator and turn the temperature to 63°C (145°F). Dehydrate until no excess liquid oozes from the pieces when torn slightly. The pieces should still be pliant.

Apricot halves can also be dried in the oven, though they can tend to burn. To reduce the chance of burning, rinse the sugar syrup off the apricots then pat dry with paper towels. Put the apricots onto baking trays lined with baking paper, then place in the oven. The temperature needs to be very low, 70°C (150°F/gas ¼) at most. The apricots will take about 8 hours to dry. When using the oven to dehydrate foods, open the oven door every hour for 1 minute to allow accumulated moisture to escape, or leave the oven door just slightly ajar for the duration of the dehydrating.

Makes approximately 200g (7oz)

VARIATION
Substitute bottled apricot halves with preserved peach, pear or nectarine halves.

APRICOT FRUIT LEATHER

2½ cups **apricot pulp** (bottled or frozen)

If you have a dehydrator, spread the apricot pulp on fruit leather sheets to 6mm (¼in) thick. Turn dehydrator to 63°C (145°F) and dehydrate until no moisture spots remain. Remove from the trays and allow to cool just slightly. Roll up if desired or cut into eighths and wrap in cling film for healthy treats.

If you do not own a dehydrator, spread the apricot pulp on baking trays lined with baking paper. Dry in the oven at the lowest possible temperature, 70°C (150°F/gas ¼) at most. The fruit leather sheets will take about 3–4 hours to dry, depending on the type of apricots used. Open the oven door every hour for 1 minute to allow accumulated moisture to escape, or leave the oven door just slightly ajar for the duration of the dehydrating.

When cool, cut into strips with a pair of scissors.

Makes 3–4 fruit leather sheets

VARIATION

Use any stewed fruits to make a variety of fruit leathers. A combination of apple and rhubarb is very nice.

DRIED APRICOT AND SULTANA CAKE

60g (2¼oz/¼ cup) butter, chopped
1 cup sugar
¾ cup sultanas
1¼ cups chopped **dried apricots**
¾ cup boiling water
1 egg, lightly beaten
2 cups self-raising flour
¼ cup lemon juice
finely grated zest of 1 lemon

Lemon icing
1½ cups icing sugar
2 teaspoons butter
2 tablespoons lemon juice, approximately

Grease a 20cm (8in) square cake tin and line the base with baking paper.
Grease again. Preheat the oven to 170°C (325°F/gas 3).

Place the butter, sugar, sultanas and dried apricots in a bowl and cover with
the boiling water. Stir well to combine, then set aside to cool.

Whisk the egg, and then add it along with the flour, lemon juice and zest into
the cooled butter mixture. Mix until well combined. Pour into the greased tin
and bake for 30 minutes, or until a metal skewer inserted into the centre of
the cake comes out clean.

The cake is nice eaten as is, or sliced and spread with a little butter. If
you wish, spread with a little lemon icing. Place the icing sugar in a small
bowl. Stir in the butter and enough lemon juice until it becomes a smooth
spreadable consistency.

Serves 8

Cornflake Cookies

—◦

Our children caught buses to school and claimed they felt motion sick if they ate breakfast. In those days before muesli bars, they would take these biscuits to eat when they arrived at school. I would like to have thought that they would eat a piece of fresh fruit, but the reality was they didn't, so these were a compromise—cereal and fruit in a biscuit.

125g (4½oz/½ cup) butter, softened
½ cup sugar
2 teaspoons golden syrup
1 egg
½ teaspoon vanilla extract
1 cup self-raising flour
1 cup chopped **dried apricots**
½ cup chopped pecans (optional)
2 cups cornflakes, approximately

Preheat the oven to 160°C (315°F/gas 2–3). Line two baking trays with baking paper.

Cream the butter, sugar and golden syrup in a medium bowl. Add the egg and vanilla and whisk until well combined. Mix in the flour, dried apricots and pecans, if using. Allow to stand for a few minutes. Place cornflakes in a small mixing bowl. Drop dessertspoonfuls of the biscuit mixture into the cornflakes, roll and shape into balls.

Place on the lined trays, allowing room for spreading, and cook for 12–15 minutes or until golden. Cool on wire racks and store in airtight containers.

Makes 24

Hint: *Commercial dried apricots are quite acceptable in these biscuits.*

FRUIT BUNS

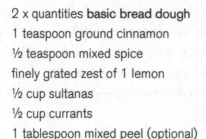

2 x quantities **basic bread dough**
1 teaspoon ground cinnamon
½ teaspoon mixed spice
finely grated zest of 1 lemon
½ cup sultanas
½ cup currants
1 tablespoon mixed peel (optional)

Place the bread dough on a lightly floured bench and knead in the cinnamon, mixed spice and lemon zest. Place the dough in a bowl and cover with a tea towel. Place the bowl in a warm place and allow the dough to rise until it has doubled in size.

Turn out the dough onto a lightly floured bench and knead for 3 minutes, or until smooth. Shape the dough into a large disc and sprinkle on the sultanas, currants and mixed peel. Briefly knead the dough to distribute the fruit evenly. Take heaped tablepoons of dough and shape each into a round ball. Place dough balls side by side, allowing 1cm space between, on a baking tray lined with baking paper. Set aside to rise in a warm place for 20 minutes or until doubled in size.

Meanwhile, preheat the oven to 200°C (400°F/gas 6).

When the buns have risen, bake for 5 minutes. Reduce the oven temperature to170°C (325°F/gas 3) and bake for a further 10 minutes or until golden brown. Transfer onto a wire rack to cool. If desired, glaze while still hot (see apricot glaze for **chelsea scrolls** on page109).

Makes approximately 8

TABBOULEH

1 cup couscous

1 cup boiling water

½ Lebanese cucumber, peeled, halved lengthways
and deseeded

½ small red onion, peeled and finely chopped

1 tomato, seeds removed, finely chopped

¼ cup finely chopped parsley

¼ cup finely chopped mint

¾ cup chopped **dried apricots**

¼ cup olive oil

¼ teaspoon sugar

2 tablespoons lemon juice

Place the couscous in a heatproof bowl and pour on the boiling water. Cover with a plate, set aside for 10 minutes, then fluff with a fork. Cover with the plate again and allow to cool completely.

Finely chop the cucumber.

Stir the cucumber, onion, tomato, parsley, mint and dried apricots into the couscous.

Whisk the oil, sugar and lemon juice in a small bowl until well combined. Mix through the couscous. Add salt and pepper to taste. Leave to stand for a few minutes to allow the flavours to develop.

Serves 4

APRICOT CHUTNEY

1.5kg (3lb 5oz) apricots, stoned and chopped
500g (1lb 2oz) onions, peeled and chopped
2 cups white or cider vinegar
750g (1lb 10oz) sugar
1 teaspoon salt
1 teaspoon ground nutmeg
1 teaspoon mixed spice
1 teaspoon ground cloves
½ teaspoon cayenne pepper
1 teaspoon curry powder

Combine all the ingredients in a large saucepan over medium heat and bring to the boil, stirring until the sugar dissolves. Reduce heat to medium–low and simmer steadily, stirring regularly, for 1 hour or until the chutney has thickened.

Pour into sterilised bottles and seal immediately. The chutney can be eaten at once.

Store in a cool, dry and dark place for up to 2 years. Refrigerate after opening.

Makes approximately 2kg (4lb 8oz)

CRUMBED CHICKEN WITH SPICED APRICOT CREAM

My daughter Stephanie mixes apricot chutney with sour cream as an accompaniment to crumbed chicken fillets. She is gluten intolerant and uses gluten-free cornflour in place of the flour and gluten-free cornflakes (that she turns into crumbs in the food processor) in place of the breadcrumbs. She uses cider vinegar in the **apricot chutney** recipe.

SPICED APRICOT CREAM
½ cup sour cream
1 tablespoon **apricot chutney** (or to taste)

2 skinless chicken breast fillets, cut in half
1 egg
2 tablespoons plain flour
1½ cups dried breadcrumbs, approximately
canola or peanut oil, for frying

For the spiced apricot cream, combine the sour cream and apricot chutney in a small bowl and set aside.

Pound the chicken fillets with a meat mallet until 1cm (½in) thick.

Lightly beat the egg with a fork in a shallow bowl. Place the flour in another shallow bowl and the breadcrumbs in a third bowl.

Dip the chicken pieces, one at a time, first in the flour, then in the egg and finally in the breadcrumbs. It's a little messy—I use one hand for the flour dipping, then the other for the egg and breadcrumbs. Transfer to a tray and place in the fridge for 30 minutes to set the coating.

Heat the oil to a depth of 1cm (½in) in a large frying pan over medium heat. Add the crumbed fillets and cook for about 3 minutes or until golden brown, on each side. Remove from the pan and place on crumpled paper towel to drain.

Serve with the spiced apricot cream and seasonal vegetables or a simple green salad dressed with a little **cherry vinegar.**

Serves 4

Rich Pasta Sauce

1 tablespoon olive oil

250g (9oz) beef mince

250g (9oz) pork mince

1 onion, peeled and finely chopped

3 garlic cloves, peeled and crushed

¼ cup red wine

1 tablespoon soy sauce

3 teaspoons Worcestershire sauce

1½ teaspoons brown sugar

1 tablespoon **apricot chutney**

2 heaped tablespoons tomato paste

1½ cups tinned or **bottled tomatoes**

½ cup beef, chicken or vegetable stock or water

2–3 teaspoons cornflour mixed to a paste with a little
    cold water

Heat the oil in a saucepan over medium–high heat and brown the beef
and pork mince, stirring constantly. Stir in the onion and garlic and cook for
1 minute. Add the red wine, soy sauce, Worcestershire sauce, brown sugar,
apricot chutney, tomato paste, tomatoes and stock or water. Bring to the
boil and add salt to taste. Reduce heat to low and simmer uncovered for
30 minutes, stirring occasionally. Thicken, if necessary, with some or all of
the cornflour paste. Serve over pasta, gnocchi or jacket potatoes.

Makes approximately 750ml (26fl oz)

TANGY AND DELECTABLE MEAT PIE

1 tablespoon olive oil

500g (1lb 2oz) beef mince

1 onion, peeled and finely diced

1 carrot, peeled and finely diced

1 celery stalk, finely diced

2 teaspoons Worcestershire sauce

3 teaspoons **apricot chutney**

2 teaspoons soy sauce

1 cup water

1 teaspoon salt

3 teaspoons cornflour mixed to a paste with a little
cold water

1 sheet frozen puff pastry, thawed

Heat the oil in a medium saucepan over medium–high heat and brown the mince, stirring often. Add the onion, carrot and celery and cook for 5 minutes. Add the Worcestershire sauce, apricot chutney, soy sauce and water and cook, stirring occasionally, for 20 minutes. Thicken, if necessary, with some or all of the cornflour paste.

Preheat the oven to 200°C (400°F/gas 6).

Pour the beef mixture into a 20cm (8in) deep-sided pie or casserole dish. Top with puff pastry, folding in the edges to fit the dish, and prick with a fork in several places. Bake for 20 minutes or until the pastry is puffed and golden.

Serves 4–6

VARIATIONS

Individual meat pies

Spoon meat mixture into 1-cup capacity pie dishes. Cover with pastry trimmed to the edge. Bake in a 200°C (400°F/gas 6) preheated oven for 15–20 minutes or until the pastry is puffed and golden.

Cottage pie

Place the beef mixture in a casserole or pie dish. Cover generously with a layer of hot mashed potato and sprinkle with grated cheddar cheese. Bake in a 180°C (350°F/gas 4) preheated oven until the cheese is melted and light golden.

APRICOT JAM

———

1.5kg (3lb 5oz) apricots, halved and stones removed,
    cut into 8mm (⅜in) dice
juice of 2 lemons
¾ cup water
1.5kg (3lb 5oz) sugar

Grease a large saucepan with butter to help prevent the jam from catching on the base of the pan. Add the apricots, lemon juice and water and cook over medium heat, stirring often, until the apricots are tender.

Add the sugar and bring to the boil, stirring. Reduce heat to medium and cook for about 20 minutes, stirring regularly, until the jam has reached setting point. To test if jam is set, place 2 teaspoons of the mixture onto a cold saucer and place in the fridge for 5 minutes. Run your finger through the cold jam. The jam has reached setting point if the surface is quite firm and wrinkles when you pull your finger through it.

Pour the jam into warm, sterilised jars and seal immediately. The jam can be eaten as soon as it cools.

Store for up to 12 months in a cool, dry and dark place. Refrigerate after opening.

Makes approximately 2kg (4lb 8oz)

Hint: *Apricot jam can sometimes discolour on the shelves. This can be prevented by placing the jars of jam in the freezer. The jam doesn't freeze because of the high sugar content, and will always keep its bright colour and flavour. (This also applies to raspberry jam.)*

CHELSEA SCROLLS

2 x quantities **basic bread dough**
1 ½ tablespoons butter, approximately
¼ cup brown sugar, firmly packed
1 ½ teaspoons ground cinnamon
finely grated zest of 1 lemon
1 cup sultanas
½–¾ cup **apricot jam**

Follow the basic bread dough recipe and let the dough rise once. Turn the dough out onto a lightly floured bench and knead until smooth.

Preheat the oven to 190°C (375°F/gas 5). Line a baking tray with baking paper.

Shape the dough into a rectangle, approximately 1.5cm (⅝in) thick, spread with the butter and sprinkle on the sugar, cinnamon, lemon zest and sultanas. Roll up, Swiss-roll style, and cut into 3cm (1¼in) slices. Place, cut side up, side by side on the lined tray. Set aside for 15–20 minutes, or until doubled in size.

Bake the scrolls for 15 minutes, or until golden brown.

Meanwhile, warm the apricot jam in a small saucepan over low heat, then sieve. Glaze the tops of scrolls while hot with the apricot jam. Transfer to a wire rack to cool. Serve warm or cold.

Makes approximately 8

JAM DROPS

This recipe is an excellent way to utilise jam that has set too firmly. I generally use **apricot jam** as it combines well with the lemon in the biscuit dough. Of course, any jam can be substituted for the apricot.

When the jam is cooked in the biscuit, it turns into a tasty lolly-like treat, popular with old and young alike.

> 125g (4½oz/½ cup) butter, softened
> ¾ cup sugar
> 2 eggs
> 2 teaspoons finely grated lemon zest
> 2 cups self-raising flour
> 1 cup desiccated coconut, approximately
> ½–¾ cup **apricot jam**

Preheat the oven to 160°C (315°F/gas 2–3). Line three baking trays with baking paper.

Whisk the butter and sugar in a medium bowl. Add the eggs and lemon zest and whisk until well combined. Add the self-raising flour and mix to form a soft dough with a metal spoon. Set aside to stand for 10 minutes.

Place the coconut in a shallow bowl. Form the dough into walnut-sized balls and roll in the coconut. Place on the lined trays, allowing room for spreading. Press your thumb into the top of each biscuit, making a generous indent (do not go right through), and fill each with a little of the apricot jam. Bake for 15 minutes, or until lightly browned. Transfer the biscuits to a wire rack to cool.

Makes approximately 24 biscuits

Hint: *Avoid using jam that is soft set, as it will leach out onto the biscuits.*

OLD-FASHIONED CURRIED SAUSAGES

500g (1lb 2oz) sausages
1 tablespoon peanut, canola or light olive oil
1 onion, peeled and finely chopped
1 carrot, peeled and finely chopped
1 celery stalk, finely chopped
½ parsnip, peeled and finely chopped
2 teaspoons curry powder
1 dessertspoon **apricot chutney**
1 dessertspoon soy sauce
1 dessertspoon Worcestershire sauce
3 teaspoons **apricot jam**
1 dessertspoon **sweet chilli sauce** (optional)
3 cups water
4 teaspoons cornflour mixed to a paste with about
    ¼ cup cold water

Prick the sausages and place in a large saucepan. Add enough cold water to cover and bring to the boil. Reduce the heat to low and cook for 3 minutes. Drain and set aside to cool. Remove the sausage skins, if desired. Cut the sausages into 2cm (¾in) lengths.

Heat the oil in a large saucepan over medium heat. Add the vegetables and sauté for 5 minutes or until almost tender. Add the curry powder and cook for 1 minute. Add the apricot chutney, soy sauce, Worcestershire sauce, apricot jam, sweet chilli sauce, if using, and the water. Bring to the boil and then simmer for 15 minutes. Thicken with some or all of the cornflour paste. Add the sausages and simmer for a further 2 minutes, stirring, adding salt and pepper to taste. Serve with steamed rice, pilaf or mashed potatoes.

Serves 4–6

SPOONER PIE

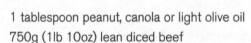

1 tablespoon peanut, canola or light olive oil

750g (1lb 10oz) lean diced beef

2 onions, peeled and finely chopped

2 teaspoons curry powder

½ red capsicum, finely chopped

2 carrots, peeled and thinly sliced

1 parsnip, peeled and thinly sliced

2 teaspoons soy sauce

2 teaspoons Worcestershire sauce

1 tablespoon **apricot jam**

2 teaspoons chutney

1 teaspoon salt

1½ cups beef or vegetable stock, or water

4 teaspoons cornflour mixed to a paste with ¼ cup
    cold water

1 sheet frozen puff pastry, thawed

Heat the oil in a large saucepan over medium–high heat, add the beef
and sauté until browned. Stir in the onion and curry powder and sauté for
2 minutes. Add the capsicum, carrot, parsnip, soy sauce, Worcestershire
sauce, apricot jam, chutney, salt and stock or water. Bring to the boil, reduce
heat to low and simmer for 1½–2 hours or until the meat is very tender.
Taste and season with extra salt, if necessary. Thicken with the cornflour
paste, noting that you may not need to use it all.

Preheat the oven to 200°C (400°F/gas 6). Pour the meat mixture into
a casserole dish. Place the pastry on top and prick with a fork in several
places. Bake for 20 minutes, or until the pastry is puffed and golden.

Serves 4–6

STEAMED APRICOT PUDDING

1 egg
½ cup sugar
1½ cups self-raising flour
½ cup milk
½ teaspoon vanilla essence
90g (3¼oz) butter, melted
3 tablespoons **apricot jam**

Grease a 4-cup capacity pudding basin.

Whisk together the egg and sugar, then whisk in all at once the flour, milk, vanilla essence and butter until the mixture is very smooth.

Place the apricot jam in the base of the pudding basin and pour the pudding mixture over. Cover the basin with its lid, if it has one, or with a piece of greased aluminium foil (greased-side down) and crimp to edges.

Place the pudding basin in a large saucepan and pour boiling water around the outside of the basin to half way up its sides. Cover saucepan with lid and bring to the boil over medium–high heat, then reduce heat to low and simmer for 1½ hours. Remove the pudding from the saucepan and allow basin to stand for 3–5 minutes, then turn out onto a serving dish. Serve with custard and ice cream, or cream.

Serves 6

VARIATION
Add a ¼ cup finely chopped glace ginger to the pudding batter, or substitute I tablespoon ginger preserved in syrup, chopped, for I tablespoon of the apricot jam.

BERRIES

Near our home on the Tasman Peninsula the berry season is always eagerly anticipated. Not long before Christmas the peninsula's magnificent berries start to ripen. Our friend, Cliff, has a small property in a fertile valley near a township called Koonya.

He takes fierce pride in his organically grown berries, and for good reason. Lovingly tended and fed by a mineral spring on the farm, they are bursting with flavour. Every day during the summer youngberries, raspberries, strawberries, tayberries, silvanberries and many others can be purchased from a shaded roadside stall. Plaited strands of deep purple garlic hang from the roof and poles of the stall or are heaped in baskets on the ground below and freshly dug pink-eye potatoes are piled high on the tables.

Cliff has no real aspirations for his produce to be a great money-making venture, but rather loves to share the berry experience with the locals and tourists who line up to sample and purchase his wares.

The property itself is well worth a visit. A ramshackle old house, that serves as a storeroom and is over 100 years old, is nestled near the base of an enormous oak tree. Cliff tells me that four people can link hands around the tree's girth. On the hottest summer's day, stepping under its branches is like entering a cool and shady glen in the midst of a berry paradise.

BOTTLED BERRIES

2kg (8lb 4oz) berries, any type
preserving syrup of choice

Place the sealing rings on clean preserving jars. Spoon the berries into the jars and fill to the brim with the sugar syrup of choice (see below). I usually use light syrup or water:

light syrup: one part sugar to four parts water
medium syrup: one part sugar to two parts water
heavy syrup: equal parts sugar and water

I make this syrup up in a plastic jug. For heavy syrup, half fill the jug with sugar, add enough boiling water to dissolve the sugar, then fill the remainder of the jug with cold water. Cool. The syrup is then ready to use.

Place the lids on the jars, secure with clips or, if using screw-top jars, screw on the lids. Transfer the jars to the preserving outfit. Fill preserver with cool water to just cover the lids. Bring to 95°C (203°F), making sure that this takes at least 1 hour. Hold at this temperature for 30 minutes for jars containing up to 10 cups of fruit with liquid. Add an extra 15 minutes for larger jars.

Remove the jars from preserver and place on a chopping board. Leave the jars to stand undisturbed for 24 hours.

Remove the clips, if using, checking that the lids are concave (this indicates that the jar is sealed). If a lid isn't concave, refrigerate the jar and use the berries within 2 days.

Makes approximately 4 x 200g (7oz) jars

Note: *Water or fruit juice can also be used in bottled berries. Very little liquid is required as the berries create their own juice.*

FROZEN BERRIES

Seasonal berries, any quantity.

Berries can be frozen very successfully.

For free-flowing berries, spread the berries in a single layer on trays and place in the freezer until just frozen. Remove from the freezer and transfer the berries to freezer containers or bags and return to the freezer.

Alternatively, and this is much easier, place the berries in freezer bags or containers and freeze in a solid pack. Always allow a little space in the top of the bag or container to allow for expansion.

I don't add sugar as the berries are used for a range of purposes. Sugar should never be added to fruit that may be later made into jams.

MERINGUE NESTS WITH BERRY COULIS

Meringue nests are an excellent standby to have in your pantry and can at a moment's notice can be filled with **crème chantilly**, mascarpone cheese or lemon curd (see Variation) and decorated with seasonal fruits.

2 egg whites
1¾ cups caster sugar
2 teaspoons white vinegar
2 tablespoons boiling water

BERRY COULIS
500g (1lb 2oz) berries
125g (4½oz) sugar (or to taste)
1 tablespoon lemon juice

1 x quantity **crème chantilly**
mixed seasonal berries

Preheat the oven to 100°C (200°F/gas ½). Line two baking trays with baking paper.

For the meringue nests, place the egg whites, sugar, vinegar and water in a bowl, boiling water last, and beat until stiff peaks form. Spoon the meringue mixture into a piping bag fitted with a star nozzle. Pipe 8cm (3¼in) rounds onto the lined trays, to form the base of the nest, then pipe on the sides. Bake for 1 hour, or until the meringue nests are crisp and dry.

For the berry coulis, place the berries, sugar and lemon juice in a saucepan over low heat. Bring to the boil and simmer for 3 minutes. Strain through a sieve. Return sieved mixture to the pan, bring back to the boil and simmer for 1 minute. Set aside to cool before using.

To assemble, place a meringue nest on a serving plate. Fill the centre with the crème chantilly and decorate with the berries. Drizzle the coulis around the nest and over the berries.

Serves 6

Hint: *Meringue nests keep well stored in an airtight container. If you have no coulis on hand, use a little cordial syrup, even a good-quality commercial blackcurrant or raspberry syrup will do.*

VARIATION (for filling)

Lemon curd

1 teaspoon cornflour
juice of 2 lemons
2 eggs, lightly whisked
¾ cup sugar
125g (4½oz) butter, chopped
very finely grated zest of 1 lemon, optional

Dissolve cornflour in lemon juice in a small bowl.

Combine the eggs, sugar, butter and lemon zest, if using, in a small saucepan. Add cornflour and lemon juice and whisk over a low heat until mixture thickens. Do not allow to boil.

Pour into sterilised jars and seal. Keep in the fridge and use within 2 weeks.

Makes approximately 2 cups

BERRY SWIRL ICE CREAM

4 eggs, separated
1 cup icing sugar
2 teaspoons golden syrup
2 cups whipped cream
½ teaspoon vanilla essence
250g (9oz) fresh, frozen or **bottled berries**
sugar (to taste)
2 teaspoons cornflour mixed to a paste with a little
    cold water

Beat the egg whites in a large bowl until stiff peaks form. Add the icing sugar and beat until stiff and glossy and the sugar has dissolved.

In a separate bowl, beat the egg yolks and syrup until well combined. Beat the egg yolk mixture into the egg white mixture. Fold in the whipped cream and vanilla essence. Pour into a 2-litre freezer container and place in the freezer until almost frozen.

Place the berries in a small saucepan and bring to the boil. Stir in the sugar and return to the boil. Mix in the cornflour paste, stirring quickly. Remove from the heat and set aside to cool completely.

Remove the ice cream from the freezer and swirl in the berry mixture. Return to the freezer to freeze completely. This ice cream is delicious served with berry coulis (see page 117).

Makes approximately 3–4 cups

BERRY SHORTCAKE

—∘

250g (9oz) butter, softened
250g (9oz) sugar
2 eggs, lightly beaten
60g (2¼oz) custard powder
200g (7oz) self-raising flour
240g (8½oz) plain flour
small amount of egg white

FILLING
500g (1lb 2oz) fresh, frozen or **bottled berries**
½ cup sugar (or to taste)
5 teaspoons cornflour mixed to a paste with ¼ cup cold water
icing sugar, for dusting

Grease a 30 x 25cm (12 x 10in) deep-sided Swiss roll tin.

For the pastry, whisk butter and sugar. Add the eggs and mix well. Add the custard powder and flours and mix with a metal spoon to form a soft dough. Wrap in cling film and place in fridge for 1 hour, or until dough is firm.

Meanwhile, place the bottled berries for the filling in a saucepan over low heat and bring to the boil. Simmer for 5 minutes, or until the berries are just cooked. Add the sugar and stir to dissolve. Bring back to the boil and thicken with the cornflour paste, a little at a time, stirring constantly. The mixture will thicken as it cools so take care not to add too much, else risk losing that wonderful berry zing. Set aside to cool. (To hasten this process, spread the filling out onto two dinner plates—it will only take a few minutes.)

Preheat the oven to 200°C (400°F/gas 6).

Divide the dough in half and roll out one portion on a lightly floured bench. Line the greased tin with dough and trim edges to fit. Brush the dough with egg white, making sure it is covered to the edge. Roll out the remaining pastry to cover the top and set aside.

Spoon the cooled berry mixture over the pastry base. Cover with the remaining piece of pastry. Trim the edges to fit neatly. Prick with a fork in several places. Bake for 5 minutes, then reduce the oven temperature to 160°C (300°F/gas 2) and bake for a further 20–25 minutes or until the crust is golden brown. Remove from the oven and allow to cool in the dish for several hours in a cool place. Dust with icing sugar and serve with thick cream and/or vanilla ice cream.

Serves 6–8

VARIATIONS
Use left-over pastry and filling mixture to make some little berry pies. Use patty pans and cook at 170°C (325°F/gas 3) for 12–15 minutes or until golden brown.

Berry meringue tartlets
Roll out the pastry to 6mm (¼in) thick and cut out 12 rounds. Line the patty pan holes with the pastry rounds and brush with egg white as for the larger pie. Place 2 teaspoons of cooled berry mixture in each tartlet case.

MERINGUE MIXTURE
2 large egg whites
½ cup caster sugar

Beat the egg whites until stiff, then add the sugar, a little at a time, and beat until stiff peaks form. Spoon or pipe the meringue mixture over the berry filling. Bake in the oven preheated at 170°C (325°F/gas 3) for 5 minutes, then reduce temperature to 150°C (300°F/gas 2) and cook for a further 10 minutes or until the crust is cooked and the meringue topping is golden.

Serves 6–8

SUMMER PUDDING

Whenever I make summer pudding it reminds me of my childhood and my grandparents' garden. My grandfather was a fractious man, autocratic to the core, as seemed to be characteristic of men of that era. In the garden, however, he was a man transformed.

Their home stood on an acre of land on the banks of the Derwent River at Rose Bay. Pop Purton had the sloping block terraced down to the water with fruit trees and berries growing in every conceivable space. I used to love visiting there and was secretly pleased that I was a bit of a favourite with him. He would spend hours taking me around the garden, sampling this and that—peaches, apricots, currants and berries—telling me how they were grown and why they were superior to those found in his neighbours' gardens. I still remember those flavours, sensational as the fruit was, plucked fresh from the trees and bushes.

He would gather the cherries that grew with joined stalks and show me how to wear them as earrings. In the quiet summer Saturday afternoons that I so often spent there, we would pick berries and take them in to Nan, who seemed to spend most of her time contentedly in the kitchen. Her parents had owned a bakery in Sandy Bay, a suburb of Hobart, and one of my favourite dishes was her summer pudding. She assured me that the best flavour was acquired by gently heating the fruit just enough to get the juices flowing and to dissolve the sugar.

Her summer puddings always reflected the best of the season and family gatherings full of fun and laughter, with Pop sitting quietly, proud of the results of his gardening. Later, he was enthusiastically vocal during the customary after-dinner game of cards among the men, while my aunts, after dutifully washing the dishes, sat and gossiped about the happenings of the past week.

> 14 thin slices white bread, crusts removed and cut in half
>   diagonally
> 1kg (2lb 4oz) fresh, frozen or **bottled berries** (include some
>   red, black or white currants if you have them)
> juice of ½ lemon
> ½ cup water
> sugar

Line a 1.5–2-litre capacity deep-sided dish with the bread, reserving some slices for the top.

Place the berries, lemon juice and water in a saucepan over low heat and cook gently until the juices are flowing. Sweeten to taste. Turn off the heat and allow mixture to cool a little, then spoon into the bread-lined serving dish, reserving about ½ cup juice from the berry mixture. Top with the reserved slices of bread, then drizzle the last of the berry juice over the top. Cover with cling film and place in the fridge for a few hours or, even better, overnight. Serve with **crème chantilly**, ice cream, mascapone or yoghurt.

Serves 6

BLACKCURRANT CORDIAL SYRUP

My first real encounter with making **blackcurrant cordial** was when my husband, Robert, made and preserved it when we were first married. For a time he had lived and worked on an apple orchard in the Huon Valley and there the orchardist's wife, who was a great preserver, showed him how to make blackcurrant syrup. He was most impressed and thereafter made it himself. Readers of *A Year in a Bottle* may recall my scepticism at his efforts and my later astonishment when I actually tasted it and found how wonderful the flavour was.

During the time that our children were quite young, we still used the ancient recipe that my husband used when we were first married. The children helped, of course, but given the generous amounts of fruit we had to process, it was hardly surprising that they were less than impressed with the process at times.

The neighbourhood children loved to come and visit. The kitchen was a unique sight with a broom handle strung between two chairs and muslin bags of cooked and cooling blackcurrants dripping that exquisite juice into bowls below. They begged to help, and so, after significant hand-scrubbing, they would be able to squeeze the bags. This was not really necessary for extracting the juice, nor even recommended for that matter, but they loved to feel the warm fragrant juice pour over their stubby little fingers. At the end of the day we'd give them a bottle of the syrup to take home to their families as payment for all their hard work.

In more recent times I have streamlined the process and now use a different method and combination of ingredients that removes the necessity to preserve by the water bath method that Robert first used. I extract the juice far more quickly by pouring the blackcurrant mixture into a colander, and the resulting strained juice through a muslin-lined sieve. Still, I sometimes miss the sight of those muslin bags dripping in the kitchen, and the sound of small children's laughter as they delighted in the cordial making.

To this day it is not unusual for us to acquire 30kg (66lb 10oz) of blackcurrants each year. The cordial-making process can be spread over several weeks as often I just freeze a portion of the blackcurrants until I have the time and inclination to process them.

The cordial is a wonderfully refreshing cold drink used in the proportion of part cordial to 4 parts water. To relieve the symptoms of a cold or the flu, it has been used for generations as a healthy, soothing drink by simply adding boiling water, instead of cold, and drinking while still as hot as possible.

> 3kg (6lb 12oz) blackcurrants
> 12 cups water
> sugar
> 1 heaped tablespoon tartaric acid

Place the blackcurrants and water in a very large saucepan over medium heat. Bring to the boil, reduce heat to low and barely simmer for 15 minutes. Strain through a colander, then strain the resulting liquid through a sieve lined with muslin.

To each cup of liquid, add 1 cup of sugar. Place the liquid and sugar in the cleaned saucepan over low heat. Bring to a bare simmer and cook for 2 minutes. Add the tartaric acid and mix well. Pour into sterilised bottles and seal immediately. The cordial can be consumed straight away. Refrigerate after opening.

Makes approximately 6 litres (210 fl oz)

JELLY CAKES

This twist on an old-fashioned favourite takes the flavour to a whole new level, courtesy of the addition of blackcurrant cordial.

85g (3oz) packet raspberry jelly crystals

1 cup boiling water

2 tablespoons **blackcurrant cordial syrup**

1 egg

¾ cup sugar

1½ cups self-raising flour

¾ cup milk

60g (2¼oz/¼ cup) butter, melted

250g (9oz) desiccated coconut

½ cup berry jam, any kind, approximately

1 x quantity **crème chantilly**

Combine the jelly and boiling water in a shallow heatproof bowl and stir until the crystals have dissolved. Add the blackcurrant cordial syrup and mix well. Set aside to cool, but not set.

Preheat the oven to 170°C (325°F/gas 3). Grease 2–3 12-hole scoop patty pans.

Whisk the egg and sugar together until light and fluffy. Add the flour, milk and butter all at once and whisk until smooth. Place 2 rounded teaspoons of the mixture in each greased patty pan. Bake for about 10–12 minutes or until lightly golden. Allow to stand for 3 minutes, then remove from the pans and place on a wire rack to cool.

Place the coconut into a bowl. Roll the cakes briefly in the jelly mixture, then in the coconut. Transfer to the wire rack to set.

Just before serving, split the cakes not quite all the way through, spread a little berry jam inside, then add a little crème chantilly.

Makes 28

Hints: *If you prefer not to use commercial raspberry jelly, try using the preserving liquid drained from some bottled cherries, berries or even some dark grape juice. For each cup of liquid, you will need 3 teaspoons gelatine powder. Sprinkle the gelatine over the cold cherry or berry liquid or grape juice. Heat the mixture over a medium heat, stirring constantly, until the gelatine is completely dissolved and the mixture is just below boiling point. Set aside to cool (but not set). The blackcurrant cordial syrup should still be added for extra flavour.*

The colour of the coating on the cakes may not be as intense as it would be if using raspberry jelly crystals, but then you won't have any artificial additives. I have trialled this recipe using all three for comparison with some willing test taster, who unanimously voted for the natural coatings because of their more intense flavour.

VARIATION

Butterfly cakes

These are always popular. For adults, the wonderful flavour of the butterfly cakes often brings back memories of childhood parties, and they are as well received by children today as they always have been.

For decoration, make 1 cup red jelly as for the jelly cakes and about 1½ cups **crème chantilly.**

Line 24 (¼-cup capacity) muffin holes or 12 (½-cup capacity) muffin holes with paper cases and fill two-thirds full with the cake mixture. Bake in a 170°C (325°F/gas 3) preheated oven for 12–15 minutes until they are light golden brown, or until a metal skewer inserted into the centre of the cake comes out clean. Transfer cakes to a wire rack to cool.

When cold, cut a disc from the top of a cake and slice the disc in half to make the butterfly wings. Fill the indentation in the cake with **crème chantilly** and place the 2 wings on top, leaving a small space between them. Fill the space with a little red jelly. Repeat for the remaining cakes. Dust with icing sugar and serve.

Makes 24 cup cakes or 12 muffins

BLACKCURRANT MOCKTAIL

¼ cup **blackcurrant cordial syrup**
2 teaspoons lemon juice
2 teaspoons crushed ice
¾ cup lemonade or soda water
1 strawberry, hulled
1 mint sprig

Pour the blackcurrant cordial syrup into a tall glass and add the lemon juice and ice. Pour the lemonade or soda water down the inside of the glass. Stir gently.

Slit the strawberry almost in half lengthways, then slide over the rim of the glass. Decorate with the mint and serve.

Serves 1

STRAWBERRY MUFFINS WITH BLACKCURRANT SAUCE

3 cups self-raising flour
1½ teaspoons baking powder
½ teaspoon ground cinnamon
1 cup sugar
3 eggs, lightly whisked
¾ cup milk
2 tablespoons lemon juice
125g (4½oz/½ cup) butter, melted
1 cup strawberries, hulled and chopped
¼ cup **blackcurrant cordial syrup**, plus extra for drizzling
icing sugar, for dusting

Preheat the oven to 190°C (375°F/gas 5). Line 15 (½-cup capacity) muffin holes with paper cases.

Combine the flour, baking powder, cinnamon and sugar in a large bowl.

In a separate bowl, add the eggs, milk, lemon juice and melted butter and lightly whisk. Add to the dry ingredients and whisk until just combined. Do not over mix. Fold in the strawberries, then spoon into the paper cases to two-thirds full with a slight indent in the top. Drizzle ¼ teaspoon of cordial syrup over the centre of each muffin. Bake for 15 minutes or until a metal skewer inserted into the centre of the muffin comes out clean. Remove from the tins and place on a wire rack to cool.

To serve, peel off the paper cases and dust the muffins with icing sugar. Place on serving plates and drizzle with a little extra blackcurrant cordial. Serve with **crème chantilly** or crème fraiche.

Makes 15

KANGAROO PATTIES WITH BLACKCURRANT JUS

375g (13oz) good-quality beef mince
375g (13oz) kangaroo mince
1 onion, peeled and finely chopped or grated
1 egg, lightly beaten
1 cup fresh breadcrumbs
2 teaspoons Worcestershire sauce
2 teaspoons soy sauce
2 teaspoons **blackcurrant cordial**
1 tablespoon **tomato sauce**
1 teaspoon salt
4 tablespoons canola or peanut oil

BLACKCURRANT JUS
¼ cup red wine
2 teaspoons tomato paste
3 teaspoons **blackcurrant cordial syrup**
1½ cups beef stock or water
3 teaspoons cornflour mixed to a paste with a little
   cold water

Place the beef and kangaroo mince, onion, egg, Worcestershire sauce, soy sauce, blackcurrant cordial syrup, tomato sauce and salt in a large bowl and mix until well combined. Shape the mixture into patties with wet hands.

Heat the oil in a large frying pan over medium–high heat. Add the patties, in batches, and cook for 4 minutes. Turn and cook for a further 3 minutes or until just cooked through. Reduce the heat if the patties brown too quickly. Drain the patties on crumpled paper towel. Keep warm.

To make the blackcurrant jus, drain any fat from the pan and return to the heat. Pour in the red wine and stir to deglaze the pan. Add the tomato paste, cordial syrup and stock or water and stir well. Strain if desired, return to the pan and bring to the boil. Thicken with some or all of the cornflour paste. Add salt and pepper to taste.

Serve the patties with seasonal vegetables, creamy mashed potatoes and a little of the blackcurrant jus.

Serves 4

CHERRIES

On the outskirts of Richmond, a pretty historic township in the Coal River Valley, there are some wonderful cherry and apricot orchards. One of these cherry orchards belongs to Chris Wisbey and his wife, Sally. Each year we are invited to visit and pick cherries for preserving. The many varieties of sweet cherries grown here are outstanding to say the very least—huge, full of flavour, bursting with juice.

Our favourite among all the rest are the Morello cherries. Spurned by some—who really don't know what a treasure they are missing—for being too sour, these cherries have a multitude of uses. There are four Morello cherry trees in Chris's orchard and all are prolific bearers. Chris tells us that it is common for each one to produce 30kg (66lb 10oz) of cherries, so you can imagine our delight when each year we are invited to pick all we need.

Morellos make wonderful pies before they even make it to the preserving jars, and are especially suited to cherry meringue pies where the sugary meringue perfectly balances the tartness of the Morellos. They also make an exceptional fruit cordial and cherry vinegar. Bottled in sugar syrup, they look like layered jewels on the shelf; the liquid takes on the colour of the fruit, and the cherries peek out delicately from their scarlet surrounding.

Sweet cherries bottle really well and also make an excellent fruit vinegar, which makes an impressive salad dressing in its own right. A year or two ago after a season of exceptional abundance, Chris and Sally decided to make a huge quantity of cherry vinegar. An aged oak barrel was purchased especially for the purpose of storing and aging the product. The excess cherries from the commercial harvest were stored in a large freezer until there was time enough to embark on the project. A nearby commercial kitchen was hired and the cherries duly soaked in vinegar for a week in large plastic barrels. At the end of the week's soaking, we returned with great enthusiasm for the processing. However, not all went according to plan. The weather had been quite cool, so some of the cherries were still frozen—a potential disaster as a warmer temperature is preferable for maximum extraction of the juice. Committed to the point of no return, we proceeded anyway. But I had forgotten to bring the requisite muslin, purchased especially for the exercise. A desperate phone call to our home at Eaglehawk Neck meant that Robert had to drop everything he was doing and bring it to us.

Meanwhile, after boiling up about 200 kg (440lb) of cherries, we realised that this was quite a significant undertaking and had visions of being there for a week. Pastry chef son, Alistair, arrived to lend an expert hand, as did Robert with the muslin and another friend or two to help out. The mess was extraordinary but we began to make progress at last.

The kindly owners of the kitchen lent us a very large Brat pan that they used on occasion to make apricot jam for their café. This made things immensely easier, and by the end of the day the task was accomplished. The cherry vinegar made that autumn day is quite exceptional and improves in the barrel with each passing day.

BRANDIED CHERRIES

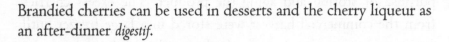

Brandied cherries can be used in desserts and the cherry liqueur as an after-dinner *digestif*.

> 500g (1lb 2oz) cherries, washed
> 125g (4½oz) sugar, or more if a sweeter liqueur is
>   preferred
> approximately 2¼ cups brandy

Prick the cherries with a fork and layer with the sugar in a sterilised jar. Pour the brandy over the cherry mixture, leaving a little space at the top of the jar. Put a lid on the jar. Shake the jar well and repeat each day for 7 days. Store in a cool, dry and dark place for 6 months.

The brandy can be strained off through a double thickness of muslin into a bottle. Keep the cherries separately with some of the cherry brandy to keep them moist. I tend to leave the cherries in the brandy and take out whatever portion of either I need at the time. This allows the flavours to continue to improve.

Makes 1.25kg (2lb 12oz) with syrup

BLACK FOREST GATEAU

This cake takes a little time to prepare, but be assured that each stage of the recipe is easy and the end result is truly worth it.

1 x chocolate cake
¼ cup cherry brandy from brandied cherries
500ml (17fl oz) crème chantilly
250g (9oz) brandied cherries, drained and pips removed
1 x quantity ganache, whipped until thickened

Cut the cake into three even layers. Place one cake layer on a serving plate and brush with half the cherry brandy. Top with a thin layer of the crème chantilly, then scatter over half the brandied cherries. Spread on another thin layer of crème chantilly and cover with a second cake layer. Brush the cake layer with the remaining cherry brandy and top with the remaining crème chantilly and brandied cherries as before. Finish with the last layer of cake. To decorate the cake, spread the ganache evenly over the top and around the sides. Place in the fridge for at least 30 minutes before serving.

Serves 8–10

BRANDIED CHERRY SAUCE

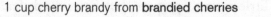

1 cup cherry brandy from **brandied cherries**
¼ cup sugar
2 teaspoons lemon juice
2 teaspoons cornflour mixed to a paste with a little cold
   water
1 cup **brandied cherries**, drained and pips removed

Place the cherry brandy, sugar and lemon juice in a small saucepan over medium heat and bring to the boil. Mix in the cornflour paste and stir until thickened. Add the brandied cherries and cook over gentle heat for 2 minutes more. Allow to cool.

Serve as a delicious topping for ice cream and panna cotta.

Makes approximately 2½ cups

CHOCOLATE CAKE WITH CHERRY BRANDY SAUCE

This recipe is very easy and so impressive.

1 x **chocolate cake**
1 x quantity **ganache**
½ cup thickened cream
½ cup **brandied cherries**, pitted and drained

Cut the cake into 8 or 12 wedges and place each slice on a serving plate. Warm the ganache until melted, then pour a little over and around each slice of cake. Place dots of cream at intervals in the ganache surrounding the cake, then drag a skewer through them, to make wonderful little white hearts in the ganache. Place brandied cherries decoratively around the cake to serve.

Serves 8–12

MINI CHERRY MUD CAKES

¾ cup **brandied cherries**, drained
2 eggs
1 cup sugar
2 tablespoons cocoa powder
1 cup self-raising flour
½ cup milk
90g (3¼oz/⅓ cup) butter, melted
icing sugar, for dusting

Preheat the oven to 170°C (325°F/gas 3). Line 24 (¼-cup capacity) patty pan holes with paper cases.

Remove the pips from the cherries and discard. Chop the cherries into halves or quarters, depending on their size.

Place the eggs, sugar, cocoa, self-raising flour, milk and butter in a large bowl and beat for 3 minutes or until light and creamy. Fold in the brandied cherries and pour the mixture into the paper cases to two-thirds full. Bake for 12–15 minutes until cooked through or until a metal skewer inserted into the centre of the cake comes out clean.

Serve cooled cakes dusted with icing sugar or top with cool, whipped **ganache** for a wonderful fudgy icing.

Makes 24

CHERRY VINEGAR

———∘

The method for making fruit vinegars is simple. In the past, sweetened fruit vinegars were used as cordial syrups. Try this with the taste buds of today, and most people will screw up their noses with distaste, most particularly children. I gave some to my children to try, one part fruit vinegar and five parts water, and it nearly turned their faces inside out.

I loathe waste, so developed recipes for using fruit vinegar, and cherry vinegar has become my personal favourite. Try using other fruit too, such as raspberries, strawberries, mulberries, blackberries or blueberries.

> 1.5kg (3lb 5oz) cherries (sour cherries if you can get them)
> 1.5 litres (52fl oz/3 cups) cider vinegar
> sugar

Mash the cherries a little to extract maximum juice and flavour. Combine the cherries and vinegar in a large glass or non-reactive bowl (vinegar may react with some metals). Stir well, cover with cling film, and leave to stand for 7 days, stirring occasionally.

On the eighth day, strain the vinegar through a colander lined with muslin into a large saucepan. To each cup of cherry vinegar add 1 cup of sugar. The amount of sugar can be reduced to ¾ cup per 1 cup vinegar if desired. Bring to the boil over medium heat and simmer for 2 minutes. Pour into warm sterilised bottles and seal. Store in a cool, dry and dark place for 1 year. The vinegar can be used immediately.

Makes approximately 4 litres (140fl oz)

CHERRY DIP WITH OLIVE OIL

½ cup **cherry vinegar**
½ cup balsamic vinegar
1 cup good quality extra virgin olive oil

Combine the vinegars in a small shallow serving bowl. Pour the oil into a separate small shallow serving bowl.

Serve as a dip with dinner rolls or bread made from **basic bread dough,** broken into bite-sized pieces.

Serves 4

CHERRY SALAD DRESSING

¼ cup **cherry vinegar**
½ cup light olive oil
1 teaspoon Dijon mustard
¼ teaspoon salt
pinch white pepper

Place all the ingredients in a jar and shake vigorously until well combined. Store left-over dressing in a jar in the fridge. The vinegar and oil will separate, but all that is needed to combine them again is to shake the jar vigorously just before using.

Makes approximately 185ml (6fl oz)

TOMATO SALSA

1 small red capsicum, deseeded and cored
750g (1lb 10oz) ripe tomatoes
1 garlic clove, peeled and crushed
½ small red onion, peeled and diced
½ cup basil leaves, chopped
1 tablespoon olive oil
2 tablespoons **cherry vinegar**

Preheat the grill to high.

Place the capsicum under the grill and cook until the skin is blackened and blistered. Wrap in cling film. Set aside for 10 minutes. Unwrap and peel, then finely dice the flesh.

Cut the tomatoes in half and remove the seeds. Finely dice the flesh.

Place the capsicum and tomato in a bowl and add the garlic, onion and basil. Leave to stand at room temperature for 15 minutes to allow the flavours to develop.

Whisk the oil and cherry vinegar in a small bowl and stir into the tomato mixture. Add salt and pepper to taste.

Serve as an accompaniment to meat, beef or poultry dishes.

Makes approximately 3 cups

MEATBALLS WITH HONEY AND CHERRY GLAZE

500g (1lb 2oz) beef, or pork and veal mince
¾ cup fresh breadcrumbs
½ teaspoon salt, or to taste
1 egg, lightly whisked
2 teaspoons **tomato chutney**
2 teaspoons Worcestershire sauce
1 tablespoon **cherry vinegar**
2 teaspoons soy sauce
1 onion, peeled and finely chopped or grated
3 tablespoons canola or peanut oil

SAUCE
½ cup water
½ cup **tomato sauce**
1 tablespoon vinegar
3 teaspoons brown sugar
2 teaspoons mild honey
2 tablespoons cherry vinegar
1 teaspoon instant coffee powder
1 tablespoon **sweet chilli sauce**
1 tablespoon lemon juice

Combine the mince, breadcrumbs, salt, egg, tomato chutney, soy and Worcestershire sauces, cherry vinegar and onion in a large bowl and mix well. Shape into walnut-sized meatballs with wet hands.

Heat the oil in a large frying pan over medium–high heat. Add the meatballs in batches and cook for 3 minutes on one side. Turn and cook for 2 minutes on the other side or until just cooked through. Drain meatballs on crumpled paper towel.

Wipe frying pan to remove any fat. Return meatballs to the pan, off the heat, while making sauce.

For the sauce, place all the ingredients in a small saucepan over medium heat and bring to the boil. Simmer for 3 minutes, then pour the sauce over the meatballs and cook over medium heat for about 5 minutes, or until the sauce is reduced a little. Add salt and pepper to taste.

Serve with fresh seasonal vegetables or steamed rice and salad.

Serves 4

RED CABBAGE WITH BACON AND CHERRY VINEGAR

Any fruit vinegar can be used in this recipe, but none is as tasty as cherry.

    1 tablespoon olive oil
    125g (4½oz) lean rindless bacon, diced
    1 onion, peeled and finely diced
    1 apple, cored and finely diced
    4 cups shredded red cabbage
    2 tablespoons **cherry vinegar**

Heat the oil in a large frying pan over medium heat. Add the bacon, onion and apple and sauté for 5 minutes, stirring often. Add the red cabbage and cherry vinegar and mix well. Reduce the heat to low, place a lid on the pan and cook, stirring occasionally, for 10 minutes or until the cabbage is tender. Remove the lid and, if any liquid remains, increase the heat to medium–high and cook until evaporated. Add salt and pepper to taste. This is delicious with pork sausages or roast pork.

Serves 4

CHILLIES

SWEET CHILLI SAUCE

Use long red chillies for this recipe. Once on radio during a 'Jams and Preserves' talkback, a gentleman rang in most disgruntled as he had made it with tiny red bird's-eye chillies. It had taken ages to chop them and the resulting sauce was way too hot to eat— admittedly my fault for not specifying initially the type of chilli to use.

250g (9oz) long red chillies, deseeded if desired and
    chopped finely
3 cups sugar
3½ cups white, cider or white wine vinegar
1 tablespoon grated green ginger
10 garlic cloves, peeled and crushed
1 teaspoon salt

Place all the ingredients in a saucepan over medium heat. Bring to the boil, stirring until the sugar has dissolved, then simmer for 30 minutes, or until the sauce has thickened slightly. Allow to stand for 10 minutes, then pour into sterilised jars and seal. The sauce can be eaten immediately. Store in a cool, dry and dark place for up to 2 years.

Makes approximately 750ml (26fl oz)

Hint: *For a slightly thicker sauce, after cooking for 30 minutes thicken with a little cornflour paste made by mixing 2 teaspoons cornflour with just a little vinegar.*

CHICKEN, BEEF OR PORK STIR-FRY

¼ cup soy sauce

¼ cup **tomato sauce**

¼ cup white, cider or white wine vinegar

1 garlic clove, peeled and crushed

1 teaspoon grated green ginger

2 tablespoons **sweet chilli sauce**

1 tablespoon honey

1 tablespoon brown sugar

750g (1lb 10oz) lean skinless chicken, beef or pork strips

1 dessertspoon canola or peanut oil

2 cups thin vegetable strips, such as onion, carrot, celery,
    capsicum, zucchini, beans, snow peas

3 teaspoons cornflour mixed to a paste with ¼ cup cold
    water (optional)

Combine the soy sauce, tomato sauce, vinegar, garlic, ginger, sweet chilli sauce, honey and brown sugar in a large bowl. Add the chicken, beef or pork, cover with cling film and place in fridge for at least 1 hour. Drain well, reserving the marinade.

Heat the oil in a large wok. Add the chicken, pork or beef and stir-fry until almost cooked through. Add the vegetables and stir-fry for 3 minutes or until just tender. Stir in the reserved marinade and bring to the boil. Thicken with a little of the cornflour paste, if desired. Serve with plain boiled or steamed rice.

Serves 4–6

Chilli Pumpkin Tartlets

These are very handy to serve as a tasty vegetarian meal or snack. The tartlets can be eaten hot or cold. Even children who dislike pumpkin will eat these quite willingly.

½ cup milk
250g (9oz) freshly grated tasty cheese
2 eggs, lightly beaten
2 tablespoons self-raising flour
1 cup cooked mashed pumpkin, cooled
1 dessertspoon **sweet chilli sauce**
2 teaspoons lemon juice
2 sheets frozen puff pastry, thawed
curried breadcrumbs

Preheat the oven to 200°C (400°F/gas 6). Grease 24 (¼-cup capacity) patty pan holes.

Place the milk in a saucepan and bring to the boil. Remove from the heat and mix in the cheese, stirring until melted. Set aside to cool for 5 minutes.

Whisk the eggs into the milk mixture. Whisk in the flour, pumpkin, sweet chilli sauce and lemon juice, then season with salt and pepper.

Cut 7.5cm (3in) rounds from the pastry. Line the greased patty holes with the pastry rounds. Three-quarters fill each pastry case with the pumpkin mixture. Sprinkle on the curried breadcrumbs. Bake for 5 minutes, then reduce the oven temperature to 170°C (325°F/gas 3). Bake for a further 12–15 minutes or until the filling is well risen and set. Allow to stand in the pans for 5 minutes then serve immediately or transfer to a wire rack to cool.

Makes 24

CHILLI CHICKEN AND CORN PARCELS

60g (2¼oz/¼ cup) butter
3 tablespoons plain flour
1 cup milk
1 cup creamed corn
½ cup freshly grated tasty cheese
1 tablespoon **sweet chilli sauce**
1 egg, lightly beaten
375g (13oz) cooked chicken meat, diced
3 sheets frozen puff pastry, thawed
tomato chutney or **zucchini pickle**, to serve

Melt the butter in a saucepan over medium heat, add the flour and cook, stirring constantly, for 1 minute. Gradually whisk in the milk and creamed corn. Bring to the boil and simmer for 3 minutes, stirring constantly. Add the cheese, sweet chilli sauce and salt and pepper to taste. Remove from the heat. Stir in the egg and chicken. Set aside to cool.

Preheat the oven to 200°C (400°F/gas 6). Line 2 baking trays with baking paper.

Cut the pastry sheets in half on the diagonal to form triangles. Place 2 heaped tablespoons of the chicken mixture on each triangle. Brush the two opposite edges of the pastry with water, then fold over to enclose the filling and form a smaller triangle. Pressing edges firmly together. Transfer parcels onto the baking trays. Bake for 10 minutes, then reduce the oven temperature to 170°C (325°F/gas 3) and bake for a further 10 minutes or until parcels are puffed and golden brown. Serve hot or cold with **tomato chutney** or **zucchini pickle**.

Serves 6

Ginger Seafood Sauce

This flavoursome sauce is excellent served with small crispy battered portions of fish.

        1 tablespoon canola or peanut oil
        4 garlic cloves, peeled and crushed
        2 tablespoons grated fresh green ginger
        2 teaspoons cornflour
        ¼ cup sugar
        ¼ cup white, cider or white wine vinegar
        ½ cup water
        1 tablespoon soy sauce
        1 dessertspoon dry white wine (optional)
        1 tablespoon **sweet chilli sauce**
        ½ teaspoon salt

Heat the oil in a saucepan over medium heat. Add the garlic and ginger and sauté for 1 minute. Stir in the remaining ingredients and cook until the sauce begins to thicken. Simmer, stirring constantly, for 3 minutes.

Makes approximately 310ml (10¾fl oz)

AUNTIE PEARL'S BATTER

Auntie Pearl, an elderly fisherman's wife from Maria Island, Tasmania, was a dear friend for many years. She told me that this recipe was the only one I would ever need for any type of seafood. I have tried many batter recipes over the past 35 years, including the usual beer and tempura variety, but true to her word, there is none better than this, the simplest of all.

1 cup self-raising flour
¼–½ teaspoon salt
good pinch of bicarbonate of soda
cold water

Place the flour, salt and bicarbonate of soda in a bowl and stir to combine. Stir in just enough cold water to make a smooth batter of coating consistency. Whisk until smooth. The batter can be used immediately, but is better if left to stand for 30 minutes.

Makes approximately 500ml (17fl oz)

Hint: *I don't restrict using this batter on fish alone. It is excellent as a crispy batter for vegetables, such as parboiled and cooled cauliflower. It can also be used to coat thin strips of pork or chicken. Unless the pieces are very small, it is generally a good idea to cook them lightly first, then cool briefly before dipping in the batter to ensure that they cook adequately.*

VARIATIONS

Crispy battered crayfish

Coat medallions of cooled cooked crayfish flesh in the batter, allowing excess to drip off. Deep fry in hot canola or peanut oil for 2 minutes, or until crisp and golden. Serve with the **ginger seafood sauce**. You'll love it.

Use any fish you like (such as flathead or ling) as a substitute for crayfish. Small fillets of fish may not necessarily need to be precooked.

If using scallops, clean the scallops and pour boiling water over them. Leave to stand for 5 minutes. Drain and pat dry with paper towel before dipping in batter.

SATAY CHICKEN

1 tablespoon canola or peanut oil

1 onion, peeled and chopped (optional)

1 garlic clove, peeled and crushed

500g (1lb 2oz) skinless chicken breast or thigh fillets,
    cut into strips

1 heaped tablespoon peanut butter

1 tablespoon **tomato sauce**

1 tablespoon soy sauce

1 tablespoon Worcestershire sauce

2 tablespoons **sweet chilli sauce**

1 cup coconut milk or water

Heat the oil in a large frying pan or wok over medium–high heat. Add the onion, if using, and sauté until soft but not browned. Stir in the garlic and cook for 1 minute. Add the chicken and cook for 5 minutes or until almost cooked through. Remove from the heat. Add the peanut butter, tomato sauce, soy sauce, Worcestershire sauce, sweet chilli sauce and coconut milk or water and stir until well combined.

Return the pan to medium heat. Bring to the boil and simmer for 7 minutes or until the chicken is tender and the sauce reduced a little. Add salt and pepper if needed. Serve with steamed rice, couscous or jacket potatoes and a salad.

Serves 4

COURTNEY'S SPICY LENTILS

¾ cup brown lentils, washed and drained
1½ cups water
1 tablespoon olive oil
1 onion, peeled and finely chopped
1 carrot, peeled and diced
2 garlic cloves, crushed
1 teaspoon ground coriander
½ teaspoon ground allspice
1 teaspoon ground cumin
1 teaspoon salt (or to taste)
2 tomatoes, chopped
1 heaped tablespoon tomato paste
1 tablespoon **tomato chutney**
¼ cup **sweet chilli sauce**

Soak the lentils in the water for at least 1 hour.

Heat the oil in a large saucepan over medium heat, add the onion and carrot
and cook, stirring occasionally, for 5 minutes or until soft. Stir in the garlic
and cook for 2 minutes. Add the spices and stir until fragrant. Add the salt,
tomato, lentils and water, tomato paste, tomato chutney and sweet chilli
sauce and stir well. Bring to the boil, reduce heat to low and simmer, stirring
often, for 50 minutes or until the lentils are tender and all the liquid has been
absorbed. Add extra salt, if needed, and pepper to taste. Serve with couscous
and **raita** or plain yoghurt. The lentils keep well, stored in an airtight container
in the fridge, for up to 3 days.

Serves 3

RAITA

½ Lebanese (short) cucumber, deseeded and coarsely grated
½ teaspoon salt
¾ cup plain yoghurt
1 spring onion, thinly sliced
1 small garlic clove, peeled and crushed
2 teaspoons lemon juice
¼ teaspoon ground cumin
1 teaspoon **sweet chilli sauce**

Combine the cucumber and salt in a bowl and set aside for 1 hour. Transfer to a colander and drain well, pressing down with a spoon to squeeze out the liquid.

Place the cucumber in a serving bowl, add remaining ingredients and mix well. Serve immediately or cover with cling film and place in fridge until required.

Makes approximately 500ml (17fl oz/2 cups)

SWEET CHILLI DIP

125g (4½oz) cream cheese, at room temperature
½ cup **sweet chilli sauce**

Place the cream cheese on a serving plate and pour the sweet chilli sauce. Serve as a dip with plain savoury biscuits, such as water biscuits or rice crackers, or chunks of crusty fresh bread.

Serves 4

CHILLI CON CARNE

1 tablespoon canola or peanut oil

3 large onions, peeled and finely chopped

6 cloves garlic, peeled and crushed

1.5kg (3lb 5oz) lean beef mince

3 tablespoons **sweet chilli sauce**

1 ½ tablespoons ground cumin

1 tablespoon dried oregano

½ cup tomato paste

500g (1lb 2oz) fresh, tinned or **bottled tomatoes**, chopped

1 cup beef or vegetable stock or water

1 tablespoon soy sauce

1 tablespoon Worcestershire sauce

1 tablespoon **tomato chutney**

1 teaspoon salt

1 x 400g (14oz) tin red kidney beans, drained

Heat the oil in a large saucepan over medium heat. Add the onion and sauté for 3 minutes or until transparent. Stir in the garlic and sauté for 2 minutes. Add the beef and cook, stirring occasionally, until browned. Add the sweet chilli sauce, cumin, oregano, tomato paste, tomatoes, stock or water, soy sauce, Worcestershire sauce, chutney and salt. Bring to the boil, reduce heat to low and simmer for 1 hour. Add the kidney beans and simmer for a further 15 minutes. Add extra salt and pepper to taste.

Serve with steamed rice, couscous, nachos or as a topping for jacket potatoes.

Serves 8

CURRY PASTE

———●

I use this curry paste and the tomato chilli chutney (opposite) for Indian style dishes. They match together perfectly in many recipes.

  ½ cup coriander seeds
  4 tablespoons cumin seeds
  2 tablespoons fennel seeds
  2 tablespoons fenugreek seeds
  2 tablespoons cardamom seeds
  1 cinnamon stick, broken into 4 pieces
  2 teaspoons dried chilli flakes
  1 tablespoon turmeric
  ½ teaspoon finely grated lemon zest
  juice of ½ lemon
  1 cup cider vinegar
  ½ cup water
  1 cup olive oil, plus extra

Dry roast the coriander, cumin, fennel, fenugreek, cardamom seeds and cinnamon in a large heavy-based frying pan until fragrant. Grind the spices in a spice grinder or mortar and pestle. Mix with the chilli flakes and turmeric. Add the lemon zest and juice, vinegar and water and stir to form a paste.

Heat the oil in a large frypan over medium heat. Add the paste and stir-fry for about 10 minutes or until all the liquid has been absorbed. Allow to cool a little, then spoon into warm sterilised jars. Pour a little extra oil over the top of the paste so that it keeps well. Store paste in the fridge for up to 1 month.

Makes approximately 500g (1lb 2 oz)

TOMATO CHILLI CHUTNEY

1½ tablespoons yellow mustard seeds

1½ cups white, cider or white wine vinegar

2.5cm (1in) piece of green ginger, peeled

20 garlic cloves, peeled

1½ cups olive oil

20 long red chillies, finely chopped and deseeded, if desired

2kg (4lb 8oz) ripe tomatoes, diced

1½ tablespoons turmeric

4 tablespoons ground cumin

1¼ cups sugar

1 tablespoon salt

Combine the mustard seeds and half of the vinegar in a non-reactive bowl and set aside to soak for at least 30 minutes. Add the ginger, garlic and remaining vinegar to the mustard seeds. Transfer to a blender or a food processor and process to a paste.

Heat the oil in a large saucepan over low heat. Add the chillies, tomatoes, turmeric and cumin and cook for 5 minutes or until the tomatoes begin to break down. Add the mustard paste, sugar and salt and simmer for at least 3 hours or until a chutney-like consistency is reached.

Pour into sterilised bottles and seal. Store in a cook, dry and dark place for 2 weeks to allow flavours to develop before using.

Makes approximately 1.25 litres (44fl oz)

Note: *You may sometimes find that a layer of oil appears on the top of the chutney. Never discard this oil as it is one of the chutney's preserving elements.*

Hint: *Once the chutney is all gone, I use the residual oil in salad dressings; as a dipper for bite-sized chunks of crusty bread; or to sauté meat, chicken or vegetables for a curry.*

HASTY CHICKEN CURRY

1 tablespoon canola or peanut oil
750g (1lb 10oz) chicken tenderloins or skinless breast
    fillets, cut into 2.5cm (1in) pieces
1 onion, peeled and finely chopped
2 garlic cloves, peeled and crushed
1 red capsicum, deseeded and finely chopped
2 tablespoons **curry paste**
3 teaspoons **tomato chilli chutney**
1 teaspoon paprika
2 tomatoes, diced
1 cup coconut milk

Heat the oil in a large frying pan over medium–high heat. Add the chicken and sauté for a 5 minutes or until almost cooked through. Add the onion, garlic and capsicum and cook for 2 minutes. Stir in the curry paste, tomato chilli chutney and paprika and cook for 1 minute. Add the tomatoes and coconut milk and cook for about 5 minutes or until the chicken is tender and the sauce reduced. Add salt and pepper to taste. Serve with steamed rice.

Serves 4–6

Sweet Potato and Chickpea Curry

1 tablespoon olive oil

1 onion, peeled and finely chopped

500g (1lb 2oz) sweet potato, peeled and diced

4 garlic cloves, peeled and crushed

2 tablespoons **curry paste**

1 tablespoon **tomato chilli chutney**

125g (4½oz) tomato paste

2 cups diced fresh, tinned or **bottled tomatoes**

¾ cup water

1 x 400g (14oz) tin chickpeas, drained

3 teaspoons cornflour mixed to a paste with a little
   cold water

2 tablespoons chopped coriander leaves (optional)

Heat the oil in a large saucepan over medium heat. Add the onion and sweet potato and sauté for 5 minutes or until the vegetables begin to caramelise. Add the garlic and cook, stirring, for 1 minute. Add the curry paste, chutney, tomato paste, tomatoes, water and chickpeas and simmer for 20 minutes or until the sweet potato is cooked. Thicken with some or all of the cornflour paste, if necessary. Add salt and pepper to taste. Sprinkle on the coriander if desired and serve with couscous.

Serves 4

VARIATION

Try adding some baby spinach leaves to the curry about 3 minutes before the end of cooking time.

SPICED CHICKEN WITH CHILLI YOGHURT

1 tablespoon canola or peanut oil

750g (1lb 10oz) skinless chicken breast or thigh fillets, cut
into 2cm (¾in) pieces

125g (4½oz) lean rindless bacon, finely chopped

1 onion, peeled and chopped

2 tablespoons **curry paste**

3 teaspoons **tomato chilli chutney**

500g (1lb 2oz) fresh, tinned or **bottled tomatoes**, chopped

2 teaspoons soy sauce

2 teaspoons Worcestershire sauce

2 tablespoons **tomato sauce**

CHILLI YOGHURT

1 cup Greek yoghurt

¼–½ cup **tomato chilli chutney**

2 teaspoons chopped fresh coriander leaves (optional)

Heat the oil in a large frying pan over medium–high heat. Add the chicken,
bacon and onion and cook, stirring occasionally, for 5 minutes or until the
onion is transparent. Add the curry paste and stir to coat, then add the
chutney, tomato, soy, Worcestershire and tomato sauces. Bring to the boil,
reduce heat to low and simmer for about 7 minutes or until the sauce is
reduced. Add salt and pepper to taste.

For the chilli yoghurt, combine the yoghurt and tomato chilli chutney in a
serving bowl. Stir in the coriander, if using. Serve the chicken with couscous
and the chilli yoghurt.

Serves 4–6

Lamb Curry

1 tablespoon canola or peanut oil
750g (1lb 10oz) lean lamb, cut into 2cm (¾ in) chunks
1 onion, peeled and finely chopped
2 garlic cloves, peeled and crushed
1 red capsicum, deseeded and diced
2 tablespoons **curry paste**
1 tablespoon **tomato chilli chutney**
1½ cups beef, chicken or vegetable stock or water
2 tablespoons **tomato sauce**
2 teaspoons soy sauce
2 teaspoons Worcestershire sauce
2 tablespoons **sweet chilli sauce**
3 teaspoons cornflour mixed to a paste with
    2 tablespoons cold water

Spiced yoghurt
¾ cup Greek yoghurt
3 teaspoons **tomato chilli chutney**

Heat the oil in a large saucepan over medium–high heat. Add the lamb, in batches, and sauté until browned. Add the onion, garlic and capsicum and sauté, stirring occasionally, for 3 minutes or until the onion is transparent. Stir in the curry paste and tomato chilli chutney and cook for 1 minute. Add the stock or water and sauces. Bring to the boil, reduce heat to low and simmer for 30 minutes or until the meat is tender. Stir in some or all of the cornflour paste, if necessary, and cook until thickened. Add salt and pepper to taste.

For the spiced yoghurt, mix the yoghurt and chutney in a small serving bowl. Serve the curry with the spiced yoghurt and boiled or steamed rice.

Serves 4–6

CUMQUATS

I think the full potential of cumquats is little recognised. They are the most attractive fruit on the bushes, little round waxy orange balls of flavour, nestled among bright green leaves. They can be used in a simple marmalade, but there is far more to the humble cumquat than this.

Our son Alistair recently returned to Tasmania after working overseas for several years as a pastry chef, not the least of these experiences as the Executive Pastry Chef to Gordon Ramsay at his New York restaurant, The London. When visiting us one day Alistair noticed a bowlful of cumquats on the bench and I suggested that I cook them in a sugar syrup. I thought that they would be delicious over ice cream or panna cotta. He, however, was adamant that the perfect way to serve them was with blue cheese. When I tried this marriage of flavours I was astounded; it was truly delicious. We were entertaining a group of friends a few days later so I took the opportunity to introduce this treat to them. They too were in raptures. So whenever I can get hold of cumquats, I preserve them this way.

Another pantry essential is cumquat brandy. It keeps for years and improves with the passing of time. The brandied cumquats can be eaten as part of a dessert, such as with ice cream, panna cotta, or crème caramel. A little chopped brandied cumquat is an interesting addition to a fruit cake.

CUMQUAT BRANDY

500g (1lb 2oz) cumquats, washed
500g (1lb 2oz) sugar
3 cups brandy

Prick the cumquats all over with a skewer or darning needle.

Place the cumquats in a sterilised 1.5-litre wide-mouthed jar. Add the sugar and brandy. Shake or stir gently each day until the sugar has dissolved.

Set aside in a cool, dry and dark place for 6 months.

Makes approximately 1.25 litres (44fl oz)

CUMQUAT COCKTAIL

Try this and you will never be content with the traditional champagne cocktail again.

1 sugar cube
6 drops angostura bitters
1½ tablespoons **cumquat brandy**
100ml (3½fl oz) sparkling white wine, chilled

Place the sugar cube in a chilled champagne flute and saturate with the bitters. Add the cumquat brandy and then carefully pour in the sparkling white wine.

Serves 1

COURTNEY'S MUD CAKE

This decadent mud cake is full flavoured and fruity, as a treat it is certainly worth the extra kilojoules.

250g (9oz/1 cup) butter
2 cups firmly packed brown sugar
1 cup water
⅓ cup **cumquat brandy**
150g (5½oz) dark cooking chocolate, chopped
2 large eggs
2 cups plain flour
1 teaspoon baking powder
¼ cup cocoa powder

Preheat the oven to 150°C (300°F/gas 2). Grease a 20cm (8in) round or square cake tin and line with baking paper, then grease again.

Combine the butter, sugar, water, cumquat brandy and chocolate in a saucepan over medium heat and cook, stirring constantly, until the chocolate has melted. Set aside to cool for 5 minutes.

Quickly whisk the eggs into the chocolate mixture. Add the flour, baking powder and cocoa and whisk to combine. Pour into the prepared tin and bake for 50–60 minutes or until just set.

Allow the cake to cool in the tin. Turn the cake out and serve with a little warmed (melted) **ganache** and a dollop of **crème chantilly**.

Serves 8

MINI CHRISTMAS PUDDINGS

500g (1lb 2oz) ready-made fruit or Christmas cake
   (commercial variety will do)
¼ cup **cumquat brandy**
4 brandied cumquats, pips removed and finely chopped
250g (9oz) white chocolate melts
½ cup glace cherries, halved

Crumble the cake into a large bowl and add the cumquat brandy. Mix well, adding a little extra cumquat brandy if necessary to moisten and hold the mixture together. Shape into walnut-sized balls and place on a tray. Leave in the fridge for about 1 hour to set. (In cooler climates, leave to set at room temperature.)

Melt the chocolate in a heatproof bowl over a saucepan of simmering water.

Spoon about ½ teaspoon of the melted chocolate over the puddings so that it resembles a topping of snow. Press half a glace cherry into the chocolate, then leave for about 20 minutes to set.

Makes approximately 24

TIPSY FRUIT AND NUT BROWNIES

125g (4½oz/½ cup) butter, softened slightly
1 cup sugar
2 eggs, lightly beaten
½ cup plain flour
3 tablespoons cocoa powder
¾ cup sultanas
½ cup chopped pecans or walnuts
2 tablespoons **cumquat brandy**

CHOCOLATE ICING
180g (6¼oz) icing sugar
1 tablespoon cocoa powder
1 teaspoon softened butter
3 teaspoons boiling water, approximately

Preheat the oven to 160°C (315°F/gas 2–3). Grease or lightly coat with cooking spray an 18 x 28cm (7 x 11¼in) slab tin and line with baking paper.

Whisk the butter and sugar in a medium bowl until pale and fluffy. Whisk in the eggs, then stir in the flour and cocoa. Fold in the sultanas, nuts and cumquat brandy until well combined. Spread evenly into slab tin, then bake for 25–30 minutes or until brownies have set. Allow to cool completely in the tin.

For the chocolate icing, place the icing sugar and cocoa in a bowl, add the butter and just enough boiling water to make a smooth spreadable paste.

Spread the chocolate icing over the brownie. Cut into squares to serve. Alternatively, I find that sprinkling sifted icing sugar over the brownie is sufficient.

Makes 12–15 slices

PRESERVED CUMQUATS

500g (1lb 2oz) cumquats
650g (1lb 7oz) sugar
1 cup cold water

Place the cumquats in a saucepan and barely cover with boiling water. Simmer very gently for 10 minutes. Drain. The cumquats should maintain their shape.

Meanwhile, combine the sugar and the 1 cup of water in another saucepan and bring to the boil, stirring until the sugar is dissolved. Place cumquats in the sugar syrup and simmer gently for 20 minutes or until cumquats are just tender but still holding their shape well.

Remove cumquats with a slotted spoon and place in warm sterilised bottles. Pour the syrup over and seal immediately. Store in a very cool, dry and dark place for up to 6 months.

Serve bottled cumquats drained of syrup with blue cheese, or with the syrup as a dessert with ice cream or mascarpone.

Makes approximately 700g (1lb 9oz) including liquid

LEMONS

PRESERVED LEMONS

Some time ago I made a batch of preserved lemons. When I took the lid off the jar after a few weeks, the aroma nearly bowled me over. Perhaps they had spoiled, I thought, so promptly returned them to the storeroom to think about them another day. Then I read that they do become strongly flavoured after preserving in salt this way. Still, it took a while for me to start experimenting with those preserved lemons, but when I did I was very pleasantly surprised at their usefulness, and now my pantry is never without them. They combine well with tomatoes and olives, and are used a great deal in Moroccan and South African cooking.

4 lemons
coarse salt
lemon juice
olive oil

Wash and dry the lemons well. Starting from the pointed end and cutting to within 1.5cm (⅝in) of the base, divide the lemons into quarters lengthways.

Place 1 tablespoon of salt in the base of a large sterilised jar. Pack about 1 teaspoon of salt into each lemon, pressing well into the cut edges. Make sure you do this on a plate so that you can capture all the juices that run from the lemons.

Pack the lemons tightly into the jar. Cover with a sprinkling of more salt. Place the lid on the jar and leave at room temperature for 4 days. The lemons should have exuded enough juice to cover the contents of the jar; if not, simply add lemon juice to cover.

Pour a thin layer of oil over the lemons, ensuring they are entirely covered. If this poses a problem, press a piece of crumpled baking paper down under the lemon juice, removing any air bubbles that may be trapped under it. The paper can be removed after a week or so and the lemons should stay submerged. If not, repeat the process.

The lemons will be ready to use in 4 weeks and will keep for at least 6 months, as long as the preserving liquid *always* covers every piece of lemon.

Makes approximately 600g (1lb 5oz)

Note: *Generally only the skin is used in cooking (rinsed) and the pith and flesh are discarded.*

CITRUS CHICKEN WITH PRESERVED LEMON JUS

1kg (2lb 4 oz) skinless chicken breast fillets
½ **preserved lemon**
½ cup basil leaves, shredded
1 garlic clove, peeled and crushed
1 cup orange juice
1 heaped tablespoon mild honey
3 teaspoons cornflour mixed to a paste with a little
    cold water

Preheat the oven to 190°C (375°F/gas 5).

Cut the chicken breasts in half and place in a flameproof casserole dish.

Rinse the preserved lemon, scoop out the inner flesh and pith and discard. Roughly chop the skin.

Combine the basil, garlic and preserved lemon skin in the bowl of a food processor and process until finely chopped. Add the orange juice and honey, process briefly, then pour over the chicken. Roast for 10 minutes, then reduce the oven temperature to 160°C (315°F/gas 2–3). Cook for 15–20 minutes, basting with the pan juices at least twice, until the chicken is cooked. Remove the chicken and keep warm.

Place the pan over medium heat and bring to the boil. Stir in some or all of the cornflour paste, if necessary, and cook until thickened. Add salt and pepper to taste. Serve with couscous and a green or Greek salad.

Serves 4–6

Lemon and Basil Pilaf

½ preserved lemon
2 tablespoons light olive oil
1 small onion, peeled and finely chopped
1 garlic clove, peeled and crushed
1 cup long-grain rice
1 teaspoon dried basil
3 cups boiling vegetable or chicken stock

Preheat the oven to 180°C (350°F/gas 4). Grease a 20cm (8in) casserole dish.

Rince the preserved lemon, scoop out the inner flesh and pith and discard. Chop the skin very finely.

Heat the oil in a saucepan over medium–low heat, add the onion and cook, stirring occasionally, for about 4 minutes or until the onion is transparent. Add the garlic and cook for 1 minute more. Add the rice and stir to coat with the oil. Stir in the preserved lemon and basil. Add the stock and bring back to the boil.

Pour into the prepared dish, cover with foil and bake for 15 minutes. Remove from the oven and carefully lift off the foil. Stir, cover with the foil again and bake for a further 15 minutes or until rice is cooked through and liquid has absorbed.

Carefully remove the foil, fluff up the rice with a fork to separate the grains. Add salt and pepper to taste. Serve with roast chicken with citrus quince jus, citrus chicken or slow roasted lamb.

Serves 4

SLOW-ROASTED LAMB WITH PRESERVED LEMON AND ROSEMARY

¼ cup olive oil

½ **preserved lemon**

2kg (4lb 8oz) leg of lamb

4 rosemary sprigs, broken into small pieces

2 garlic cloves, peeled and thinly sliced

¼ cup orange juice

¼ cup white wine

½ cup water

Preheat the oven to 180°C (350°F/gas 4). Pour the oil into a roasting tin.

Rinse the preserved lemon, scoop out the inner flesh and pith and discard. Shred the skin finely.

Wipe the leg of lamb with paper towel and place on a chopping board, fleshiest side up. Cut diamond slits into the flesh of the lamb at 1.5cm (⅝in) intervals, and insert small pieces of the rosemary, garlic and lemon.

Place the lamb in the prepared tin and roast for 10 minutes. Pour the orange juice, white wine and water around the lamb. Reduce the oven temperature to 160°C (315°F/gas 2–3) and cook, basting every 30 minutes, for 1½–2 hours or until the lamb is done to your liking.

Remove the lamb from the tin and place on a board or plate. Cover with foil and leave to stand in a warm place for 15 minutes before carving. Serve with roasted root vegetables and tomato and preserved lemon 'tagine'. You could also serve it with lemon and basil pilaf.

Serves 4–6

Hint: *If you have some **tomato chilli chutney**, use the oil from the top in place of olive oil.*

VARIATIONS

Baked vegetables

Root vegetables, such as sweet potato, chunks of pumpkin, parsnip, onions and carrots, can be roasted in the pan with the meat. Add them to the roasting tin when the lamb has been baking for about 45 minutes. Roll the vegetables in the pan juices and turn over after 30 minutes. Return to roast for a further 30 minutes or until cooked through. Remove vegetables from roasting tin as soon as they are cooked and keep warm.

Jus

A jus or gravy can be made from the delicious pan juices in the following way:

½ cup red or white wine

2 teaspoons tomato paste or **tomato sauce**

2 teaspoons **quince jelly**

1½ cups chicken or vegetable stock

3 teaspoons cornflour mixed to a paste with a little
    cold water

Pour any excess fat from the roasting tin. Place the roasting tin over low heat and add the wine, stirring quickly to deglaze the pan. Add the tomato sauce or paste, quince jelly and stock. Increase the heat to medium and bring to the boil. (Strain if a smoother jus is preferred.) Simmer for 2 minutes and stir in some or all of the cornflour paste to thicken or cook until the jus is reduced to the desired consistency. Add salt and pepper to taste.

Makes approximately 2 cups or 4–6 serves

TOMATO AND PRESERVED LEMON 'TAGINE'

This dish was put together more by accident than design when I had a little preserved lemon left over from another recipe and tomatoes and red capsicums going to waste. It is a tasty accompaniment to the **slow roasted lamb** or can be served as a stand-alone vegetarian dish with couscous flavoured with a little preserved lemon and chopped parsley.

½ **preserved lemon**

750g (1lb 10oz) ripe tomatoes, finely chopped

500g (1lb 2oz) red capsicums, deseeded and finely chopped

1 small onion, peeled and finely chopped

4 garlic cloves, peeled and crushed

1 long red chilli, deseeded and chopped (optional)

½ cup tomato paste

1 tablespoon **tomato chutney**

1 teaspoon sugar

1 teaspoon salt, plus extra

½–1 cup pitted kalamata olives (optional)

Scoop the flesh and pith from the preserved lemon and discard. Rinse. Chop the skin very finely.

Combine all the ingredients in a large saucepan over medium heat, bring to the boil and cook for 30 minutes, or until reduced to desired consistency. Add salt and pepper to taste.

Serves 6

MUSTARD SEEDS

EASY MUSTARD

¾ cup yellow mustard seeds
1 cup white, cider or white wine vinegar
2 teaspoons salt
2 teaspoons honey
2 teaspoons olive oil, plus extra 2 tablespoons

Grind the mustard seeds in a mortar and pestle or with a spice grinder.
Transfer to a mixing bowl, then mix to a paste with the vinegar, salt, honey
and 2 teaspoons of olive oil.

Spoon into small (110–120ml) sterilised jars, taking care to avoid air
pockets. Cover the top surface with a little of the extra olive oil.

If possible, store for 2 weeks before using to allow the flavours to develop.
The mustard will keep for at least 6 months in a cool, dry and dark place.
Refrigerate after opening.

Makes approximately 1½ cups

WHOLE SEED MUSTARD

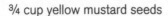

¾ cup yellow mustard seeds

1 cup white vinegar

2 teaspoons salt

2 teaspoons honey

2 teaspoons olive oil, plus extra 2 tablespoons

Place ½ cup of the mustard seeds in a bowl and cover with ½ cup of the vinegar. Cover and leave to stand for 8 hours or overnight.

Next day, grind the remaining ¼ cup of mustard seeds to a powder using a mortar and pestle or spice grinder. Transfer to a separate bowl. Pour the soaked mustard seeds into the mortar and pestle and grind only until roughly crushed. Alternatively, place the soaked seeds in a mug and process briefly with a stick blender (chopping blade attachment).

Mix the wet seed mixture with the ground mustard powder, remaining vinegar, salt, honey and 2 teaspoons olive oil. Spoon into small (110–120ml) sterilised jars, taking care to avoid air pockets. Pour a little oil over the top surface.

If possible, store for two weeks before using to allow the flavours to develop. The mustard will keep for at least 6 months in a cool, dry and dark place. Refrigerate after opening.

Makes approximately 1½ cups

EASY AIOLI

1 egg
½ teaspoon salt
1 garlic clove, peeled and crushed
1 teaspoon **easy** or **whole seed mustard**
1 tablespoon white, cider or white wine vinegar
¾ cup light olive oil

Place the egg, salt, garlic, mustard and vinegar in the bowl of a food processor and process until smooth. With the motor running, add the oil a few drops at a time. After about one-third of the oil has been added, add the rest in a slow but steady trickle. Process until thick and creamy.

Use immediately or store in a sterilised jar in the fridge, where it will keep for up to 2 weeks.

Serve with fresh, crusty bread or as part of a vegetable platter.

Makes approximately 1¼ cups

Note: *If you don't have a food processor for making aioli, whisk the egg, salt, garlic, mustard and vinegar in a bowl until well combined. Very gradually, whisk in the oil, a few drops at a time, until the mixture begins to thicken, then add the oil, still whisking constantly, in a thin stream until it is all incorporated.*

VARIATION
Omit the garlic from this recipe for a rich homemade mayonnaise.

CHICKEN AND MUSHROOM RAGOUT

1 tablespoon light olive oil

500g (1lb 2oz) skinless chicken breast or thigh fillets,
   cut into 1cm (½in) pieces

2 cups sliced button mushrooms

2 onions, peeled and finely chopped

2 garlic cloves, peeled and crushed

2 teaspoons tomato paste

2 teaspoons paprika

2 teaspoons **easy** or **whole seed mustard**

½ teaspoon salt

1 cup water

3 teaspoons cornflour mixed to a paste with a little
   cold water

½ cup sour cream (optional)

Heat the oil in a medium frying pan over medium–high heat. Add the chicken
and sauté until lightly browned. Add the mushrooms and onion and sauté for
5 minutes or until the onion is transparent. Stir in the garlic, tomato paste,
paprika, mustard, salt and water. Bring to the boil and simmer for 10 minutes.

Stir some or all of the cornflour paste into the ragout and cook until
thickened to desired consistency. Stir in the sour cream, if using, and salt and
pepper to taste.

Serves 4

VARIATION

Chicken and mushroom pie

This ragout can easily be used as a filling for a family-size pie.

Simply pour the ragout into a 20cm (8in) casserole dish and top with a sheet of thawed puff or shortcrust pastry. Prick the top of the pastry with a fork and bake in a 200°C (400°F/gas 6) preheated oven for 15–20 minutes or until the pastry is golden.

GREEN EGGS AND HAM PIE

I made up this recipe for my grandson Jacob, whose favourite book was Dr Seuss's *Green Eggs and Ham*, when he was a toddler. He just loved it—and loves it still. This pie is not just for children by the way, adults devour it too.

1 sheet frozen puff pastry, thawed, or **shortcrust pastry**
125g (4½oz) lean rindless bacon, diced
¼ small onion, grated (optional)
1 handful of baby spinach leaves, shredded
boiling water
1 cup milk
3 teaspoons cornflour mixed to a paste with a little
   cold milk
1 cup freshly grated tasty cheese
5 eggs
½ cup **pesto**

Preheat the oven to 200°C (400°F/gas 6). Grease a 20cm (8in) pie dish.

Line the prepared dish with the pastry and trim to fit, allowing the pastry to come all the way up the side of the dish. Place in the fridge while preparing the filling.

Combine the bacon and onion in a small saucepan over medium heat. Sauté for 5 minutes or until the onion is transparent and the bacon is starting to crisp. Set aside to cool.

Place the spinach in a heatproof bowl, pour on enough boiling water to cover and leave to stand for 2 minutes. Drain well, squeezing out excess liquid. Shred.

Pour the milk into a small saucepan over medium heat and bring to the boil. Add the cornflour paste and cook, stirring constantly, until the sauce comes to the boil and thickens. Remove from the heat, add half the cheese and stir until melted. Mix in the spinach and season with salt and pepper to taste. Allow to cool.

Spread a little of the spinach mixture over the base of the pastry case. Sprinkle on the bacon and onion, then dot with small mounds of the remaining spinach mixture. Break the eggs over the top and pierce the yolks with the point of a sharp knife. Place a small spoonful of pesto in each yolk, then dot half teaspoonfuls of the remaining pesto around the top of pie.

Sprinkle the remaining cheese over the pie. Bake for 8 minutes then reduce the oven temperature to 170°C (325°F/gas 3). Bake for 25 minutes or until the filling is set.

Serves 6

PESTO

This is undoubtedly one of my favourite recipes. I keep a supply of basil growing for as many months of the year as it is horticulturally possible in the hothouse, specifically to be able to keep a ready supply of pesto.

    2 cups fresh basil leaves
    ½ cup pine nuts
    2 garlic gloves, peeled and chopped
    ½ cup light olive oil
    1 teaspoon **easy mustard**
    ½ cup freshly grated parmesan cheese

Place the basil leaves, pine nuts and garlic in the bowl of a food processor and process until smooth. Keep the motor running and gradually add the olive oil. Add the mustard and parmesan and process for a few seconds more. Add salt and pepper to taste.

Serve pesto just as it is with freshly baked bread, or put a little in the centre of meatballs or a meatloaf for added flavour and interest. One of the best uses is in green eggs and ham pie.

Pesto can be stored in small air-tight containers in the freezer for up to 2 months.

Makes approximately 1½ cups

Note: *If you don't have a food processor, grind the (shredded) basil leaves, pine nuts, garlic and mustard using a mortar and pestle. Gradually mix in the olive oil until well combined, then add the mustard and parmesan. Add salt and pepper to taste.*

Mini Mustard Quiches

—◦

2 sheets frozen puff pastry, thawed

125g (4½oz) freshly grated tasty cheese

125g (4½oz) lean rindless bacon, finely chopped

3 tablespoons thickened cream or milk

2 teaspoons **whole seed mustard**

1 egg, lightly beaten

1 tablespoon finely chopped flat-leaf parsley

1 small onion, peeled and finely chopped or grated

1 teaspoon **sweet chilli sauce**

Preheat the oven to 200°C (400°F/gas 6). Grease 18 patty pan holes.

Cut 6cm (2½in) rounds from the pastry and press into the prepared patty pan holes.

Combine the cheese, bacon, cream or milk, mustard, egg, parsley, onion and sweet chilli sauce in a medium bowl and mix well.

Place a level dessertspoonful of mixture in each pastry case and bake for 12–15 minutes or until puffed and golden.

Makes 18

MUSTARD AND GARLIC BREAD

1 French stick
2 garlic cloves, peeled and crushed
1½ teaspoons **easy mustard**
125g (4½oz) butter, softened
1 tablespoon finely chopped parsley (optional)

Preheat the oven to 180°C (350°F/gas 4).

Cut the bread almost all the way through into 2cm (¾in) slices.

For the mustard and garlic butter, mix the garlic and mustard into the butter. Add the parsley, if using, and stir well.

Spread both sides of each slice of bread with the mustard and garlic butter, then place slices back together into a French stick shape again and wrap in foil. Bake for 10 minutes. Remove from the oven and open the top of the foil. Return to the oven and bake for 5 minutes or until the crust is golden and crisp.

Serves 4

Mustardy Chicken Pie

—⊃

2 tablespoons peanut or light olive oil

500g (1lb 2oz) skinless chicken thigh or breast fillets,
    cut into 1.5cm (⅝in) pieces

1 onion, peeled and finely chopped

1 carrot, peeled and diced

2 garlic cloves, peeled and crushed

1 cup fresh or frozen peas

1 cup fresh or frozen corn kernels

3 teaspoons **whole seed mustard**

½ teaspoon dried thyme

¾ cup milk

2 teaspoons chicken stock powder

3 teaspoons cornflour mixed to a paste with a little cold milk

1 tablespoon lemon juice

3 teaspoons mayonnaise

1 sheet frozen puff pastry, thawed

Preheat the oven to 200°C (400°F/gas 6). Heat the oil in a saucepan over medium heat, add the chicken, onion, carrot and garlic and sauté for 5 minutes or until the chicken is almost cooked through. Stir in the peas, corn, mustard, thyme, milk and stock powder. Bring to the boil, add the cornflour paste and stir until thickened. Stir in the lemon juice and mayonnaise. Add salt and pepper to taste.

Pour into a 20cm (8in) casserole dish and top with the pastry. Press pastry down around the edge and trim excess. Prick in several places with a fork. Bake for 10 minutes, then reduce oven to 180°C (350°F/gas 4). Cook for a further 10 minutes or until pastry is puffed and golden.

Serves 4–6

ORANGES

ORANGE MARMALADE

500g (1lb 12oz) oranges
1 lemon
4 cups water
2 cups orange juice
1.5kg (3lb 5oz) sugar

Put the fruit through a mincer or chop very finely. Place in a large saucepan, add the water and orange juice and bring to the boil. Cook briskly for about 20 minutes or until the fruit is soft. Add the sugar and bring to the boil, stirring until the sugar has dissolved. Continue to boil, without stirring, for 25 minutes or until setting point is reached (see page 18).

Allow to stand for 10 minutes then pour into warm sterilised jars. Seal immediately. Store in a cool, dry and dark place.

Makes approximately 1.5kg (3lb 5oz)

Hint: *If your children, like mine, dislike the peel in marmalade, simply sieve it out.*

BREAD AND BUTTER PUDDING

This dessert was my dad's favourite. He had a decidedly old-fashioned taste in food: meat and three vegetables were the menu options always, and dessert was an integral part of the meal. He rejected any attempt at introducing modern cuisine. The most placid of men, he nevertheless in this case stubbornly insisted that 'rice is for puddin's!' as his final word and would not compromise one jot by eating anything that resembled multicultural cuisine.

He was also adamant that currants were the only dried fruit acceptable in his bread and butter pudding. I must admit that I have used sultanas, raisins and even mixed dried fruit, but currants are by far the best.

When he came to live with us a few years after we were married, he carefully tutored me in making this bread and butter pudding until it met with his approval.

  2 teaspoons softened butter
  2 scant tablespoons **orange marmalade**
  3 slices bread, crusts removed
  ½ cup currants
  2 cups milk
  3 eggs
  ½ cup sugar
  ½ teaspoon vanilla essence
  ½ teaspoon ground nutmeg
  1½ teaspoons softened butter, extra

Preheat the oven to 150°C (300°F/gas 2). Grease a 20cm (8in) casserole dish.

Spread the butter and a thin layer of orange marmalade on the bread. Cut bread into 3cm squares. Place bread marmalade side-up in the prepared dish, overlapping if required, and sprinkle over with the currants.

Warm the milk in a saucepan over low heat until just lukewarm.

Whisk the eggs, sugar and vanilla into the milk until well combined. Pour over the bread and currant mixture. Sprinkle on the nutmeg and dot with the extra butter.

Place the casserole dish in a roasting tin. Pour enough warm water into the roasting tin to come halfway up the side of the casserole dish. Bake for 1–1½ hours or until the custard has set and the top is golden.

Serves 6

MARMALADE GLAZED CORNED BEEF

2kg (4lb 8oz) corned beef silverside

1 onion, peeled and cut in half

2 teaspoons whole cloves

1 teaspoon mixed spice or allspice berries

1 tablespoon black peppercorns

1 tablespoon dark malt or cider vinegar

1 tablespoon brown sugar

¼ cup **orange marmalade**

2 teaspoons soy sauce

½ teaspoon grated fresh green ginger (optional)

½ cup orange juice

2 teaspoons Dijon or **easy mustard**

Place the beef in a large saucepan. Add the onion, cloves, mixed spice or allspice berries, peppercorns, vinegar, brown sugar and enough cold water to cover. Bring to the boil and simmer for 2 hours or until the beef is just tender.

Preheat the oven to 170°C (325°F/gas 3).

Remove the beef from the liquid, drain and transfer to a roasting tin.

Combine the orange marmalade, soy sauce, ginger, if using, orange juice and mustard in a bowl and mix well. Pour over the beef and bake, basting every 10 minutes, for 30 minutes or until the glaze is caramelised and golden.

Cover loosely with foil and rest in a warm place for 10 minutes.

Carve into slices, dipping each slice in the juices in the tin before transferring to the serving plate. Serve with creamy mashed potato and seasonal vegetables.

Serves 6-8

GLAZED HAM

3kg (6lb 12oz) cooked leg of ham
1 cup orange or pineapple juice
whole cloves
1 cup **orange marmalade**
2 tablespoons fruit or balsamic vinegar
2 teaspoons **easy** or **whole seed mustard**
2 teaspoons **tomato chilli chutney**
1 cup orange juice, extra

Preheat the oven to 170°C (325°F/gas 3). Grease a large roasting tin.

Remove the rind from the ham. An easy way to do this is to make a small cut under the outer (widest) edge and pull back the rind with your fingers to within 5cm (2in) of the shank and cut the skin off. Discard the rind. Cut (score) a diamond pattern into the fat layer of the ham and press a clove into the centre of each diamond.

Place the ham scored side-up in the prepared tin, add the orange or pineapple juice and cover with foil. Bake for 1 hour and remove from the oven. Uncover the ham, reserving the foil.

Combine the marmalade, vinegar, mustard and chutney in a small saucepan and boil for 3 minutes. Strain if desired. Spoon the glaze over the ham and pour the extra orange juice into the base of the tin. Cover with the reserved foil and bake for 1 hour. Remove the foil and cook, basting every 15 minutes, for 1 hour or until golden brown and meat is tender.

Serves 8

HUMMINGBIRD MUFFINS

3 cups plain flour

4 teaspoons baking powder

1 teaspoon bicarbonate of soda

1 teaspoon ground cinnamon

1 teaspoon mixed spice

2 cups sugar

4 medium-sized ripe bananas, mashed

¼ cup **orange marmalade**

1½ teaspoons finely grated lemon zest

2 eggs, lightly beaten

1 cup light olive oil

250g (9oz) tin crushed pineapple in natural juice, drained

CREAM CHEESE ICING

125g (4½oz) cream cheese, softened

30g (1oz) butter, softened

1 teaspoon finely grated lemon zest

1 cup icing sugar

2 teaspoons lemon juice, approximately

Preheat the oven to 180°C (350°F/gas 4). Line 12 (½-cup capacity) muffin holes with paper cases.

Combine the flour, baking powder, bicarbonate of soda, cinnamon, mixed spice and sugar in a large bowl. Add the banana, marmalade, lemon zest, eggs, oil and pineapple and mix well. Spoon into the paper cases to two-thirds full. Bake for 15–20 minutes or until a metal skewer inserted into the centre of the muffin comes out clean. Transfer muffins onto a wire rack to cool.

For the cream cheese icing, beat the cream cheese and butter in a small bowl. Add the lemon zest and gradually mix in the icing sugar. Add the lemon juice, a little at a time, and stir until a smooth spreading consistency is reached. Spread the cream cheese icing over the cooled muffins and serve immediately or store in an airtight container in the fridge.

Makes approximately 12 muffins

Sticky Marmalade and Date Puddings

1 cup firmly packed dates, roughly chopped
¾ cup water
2 tablespoons **orange marmalade**
1 cup sugar
60g (2¼oz) butter
1 teaspoon bicarbonate of soda
1 egg, lightly beaten
2 cups self-raising flour

Caramel sauce
1 cup brown sugar
150ml (5fl oz) pouring or thickened cream
1 teaspoon vanilla extract
2 tablespoons softened butter

Preheat the oven to 170°C (325°F/gas 3). Line 12 (½-cup capacity) muffin holes with paper cases.

Place the dates, water, marmalade, sugar and butter in a saucepan over medium heat and bring to the boil, stirring often. Remove from the heat, stir in the bicarbonate of soda and set aside to cool for 10 minutes. Add the egg and flour and mix well. Spoon into the paper cases to two-thirds full. Bake for 15 minutes or until well risen and when a metal skewer inserted into the centre of the cake comes out clean. Allow to stand for 5 minutes before removing from tins.

Meanwhile, for the caramel sauce, combine the sugar, cream, vanilla and butter in a saucepan and bring to the boil. Simmer for 5 minutes, stirring frequently, until the sauce is a nice caramel colour and consistency.

Remove the puddings from the paper cases and place on serving plates. Pour a little caramel sauce over each pudding and serve with vanilla ice cream.

Makes approximately 12

Hints: *Your family possibly won't be able to eat all these at one sitting. Simply use the rest as lunch-box treats. Alternatively, freeze left-over puddings for another day.*

Any leftovers of caramel sauce can be kept to pour over ice cream. The sauce keeps well, stored in an airtight container in the fridge, for a week or two. To reheat, spoon mixture into a small saucepan and cook over low heat until it reaches pouring consistency.

VARIATION
Add a little liqueur, such as cumquat brandy (see **brandied cumquats**), for an extra citrus dimension.

PASSIONFRUIT

BOTTLED PASSIONFRUIT

1 cup passionfruit pulp (approximately 12 medium
   passionfruit)
1 cup sugar
¼ teaspoon citric acid

Combine the passionfruit pulp, sugar and citric acid in a bowl or jug. Mix well
and pour into 5 x 110ml (3 ¾fl oz) sterilised jars. Place the lids on the jars.
Leave to stand for 24 hours at room temperature, shaking the jar now and
then to dissolve the sugar.

Preserved passionfruit keeps well on the shelf in a very cool, dry and
dark place. I keep it in the fridge to be doubly sure that it will not spoil.
Alternatively you can freeze the pulp in small containers.

Note: *I don't heat the passionfruit in any way because heating tends to lessen the
wonderful intensity of the flavour.*

Makes 500ml (17fl oz)

AUNTIE VELMA'S PATTY CAKES WITH PASSIONFRUIT ICING

This recipe originated from my Auntie Velma, Dad's sister, who for many reasons was a favourite aunt. She owned a small sweet shop and milk bar on the corner of Federal Street in North Hobart, so visiting her was always special. There was more to my affection for her than this, however. When I was young she empathised with my budding compulsion to cook. Later on in life when I was to be married, she asked me what I would like for a gift. Without hesitation I replied, 'Some of your recipes!' You see she was absolutely the *best* cook. Everything was so tasty.

I couldn't wait to open her present, and she had indeed provided me with a folder of her handwritten recipes, her patty cake recipe among them. This adaptation of her original recipe is made particularly flavoursome by the simple addition of lemon and preserved passionfruit to the cake batter.

Auntie Velma had other adaptations. Always a devout Catholic, she had a speciality that she regularly made as a treat for the nuns who lived in a convent nearby (see Variation). She was always an inspiration and she would talk cooking by the hour, and it was perhaps her influence that sowed the seed for developing the full potential of flavour and ease of preparation in my recipes.

125g (4½oz/½ cup) butter, softened

1 cup sugar

2 eggs

2 cups self-raising flour

½ cup milk

2 tablespoons lemon juice

¼ cup **bottled passionfruit**
finely grated zest of 1 lemon

PASSIONFRUIT ICING
2 cups icing sugar, sifted
2 teaspoons butter, softened or melted
¼ cup **bottled passionfruit**, approximately

Preheat the oven to 170°C (325°F/gas 3). Line 24 (¼-cup capacity) muffin holes with paper cases or grease 24 patty pan holes.

Whisk the butter and sugar until pale, and then whisk in the eggs until light and fluffy. Fold in the flour, milk, lemon juice, passionfruit and lemon zest using a metal spoon until the batter is smooth. Spoon into the paper cases or pans to two-thirds full. Bake for 12 minutes until golden or until a metal skewer inserted in the centre of the cakes comes out clean.

Allow the cakes to stand in the pans for 5 minutes, then turn out onto a wire rack to cool completely.

Meanwhile, for the passionfruit icing, place the icing sugar in a bowl. Mix in the butter and a little of the passionfruit. Gradually add enough of the remaining passionfruit and stir until a good spreading consistency is reached.

Spread the icing over the cooled cakes. Leave to set.

These cakes will keep well, stored in an airtight container in a cool place, for 3 days.

Makes 18–20

VARIATION

I well remember Aunty Velma telling me how she used to make little orange cakes from the same recipe for the passionfruit. She cooked them in patty cake pans and added 3 teaspoons of grated orange zest to the mixture. After baking she iced them with orange icing, then split and filled them with sweetened whipped cream.

PASSIONFRUIT CHEESECAKE

½ batch x **sweet shortcrust pastry**

500g (1 1lb 2oz) cream cheese, softened

395g (13¾oz) tin sweetened condensed milk

½ cup icing sugar

juice of 3 lemons

3 teaspoons finely grated lemon zest

½ cup tinned or **bottled passionfruit**

⅓ cup boiling water

4 rounded teaspoons powdered gelatine

TOPPING

2 rounded teaspoons powdered gelatine

⅓ cup boiling water

1 cup tinned or **bottled passionfruit**

Preheat the oven to 160°C (315°F/gas 2–3). Grease a 23cm (9in) springform cake tin.

Roll out the pastry on a lightly floured bench to 5mm (¼in) thick. Press the pastry into the base of the prepared tin, cutting off excess to fit. Prick several times with a fork. Bake for 10 minutes, or until light golden brown. Allow to cool in a cake tin.

Combine cream cheese, condensed milk, icing sugar, lemon juice and zest and passionfruit in a bowl. Whisk until smooth.

Place the boiling water in a small heatproof bowl, sprinkle the gelatine over the top and stir briskly to dissolve. Whisk into the cream cheese mixture, then pour over the cooled base. Place in the fridge for 6 hours or until set.

When cheesecake has set, make the topping. Place boiling water in a heatproof bowl and sprinkle gelatine on top. Stir briskly to dissolve the gelatine, then stir in the passionfruit.

Pour the topping over the cheesecake filling. Return to the fridge about 1 hour or until the topping has set.

Serves 8

PASSIONFRUIT PARADISE

1½ tablespoons vodka
3½ tablespoons **bottled passionfruit**, strained
1 teaspoon lemon juice
2 teaspoons crushed ice
⅔ cup chilled lemonade or soda water
mint sprig
1 thin slice lemon

Pour the vodka into a chilled tall glass, add the passionfruit, lemon juice, ice and lemonade or soda water and stir gently. Decorate with the mint and lemon slice and serve.

Serves 1

Never-fail Pavlova with Passionfruit Coulis

This is extremely simple to make and has a crisp outer crust with a marshmallowy middle, which makes it all the more appealing.

3 egg whites
1½ cups caster sugar
1 teaspoon white vinegar
1 teaspoon cornflour
2 tablespoons boiling water
1½ cups **crème chantilly**
1 punnet fresh berries
½ cup **bottled passionfruit**

Preheat the oven to 130°C (250°F/gas 1). Line a baking tray with baking paper or grease a heatproof plate (this saves transferring the pavlova after cooking, which can be a bit tricky).

Place the egg whites, sugar, vinegar and cornflour in a large very clean bowl. Add the boiling water and beat immediately with electric beaters until very stiff. When you think you have reached this point, remove the beaters and tilt the bowl. If the pavlova mixture doesn't move, carefully turn the bowl upside down. If the mixture still keeps its shape and doesn't move, it is ready.

Pile the pavlova mixture onto the prepared tray or plate and shape into an 18cm (7in) mound with a level top. Bake for 15 minutes, reduce the oven temperature to 90°C (200°F/gas ½) and cook for a further 45 minutes. Remove from the oven and leave to cool at room temperature.

Decorate with crème chantilly and berries. Drizzle the preserved passionfruit over the top and around each slice as it is served.

Serves 6–8

QUINCES

In our house, autumn and ripening quinces are very eagerly anticipated. More than any other fruit, quinces mark the changing of the seasons. Their wonderful aroma as they cook fills the house and reminds us of the increasing chill in the morning air. The balmy autumn days are a delight after the searing summer heat.

Toffee quinces, the most traditional of all our family desserts, are prepared at this time of year. Whole quinces are cooked for about 3 hours in sugar syrup. As they cook, their outer skin begins to break down and allows the intensely flavoursome juice from the fruit to ooze into the liquid and the syrup penetrates the fruit. When the simmering time is finished, you have wonderful scarlet soft-to-the-core quince toffees, with an intensely flavoured syrup surrounding them. It is one of those desserts that is so rich you feel you can eat only a little but at the same time cannot help returning again and again for another mouthful. We have some people who visit us each autumn for the express reason of indulging in this annual treat. A bonus feature of this dish is that the syrup that remains after the quinces are lifted out is then poured into jars, where it will set into the most wonderful deep scarlet jelly in which tiny pieces of toffee quince skin or flesh are suspended—a tasty treat for fresh bread, toast or scones.

This year I watched a bumper crop ripen on a tree, which has been my most regular and prolific source of quinces, in a nearby township and anticipated this dessert once more. I could also visualise the dozens of jars of quince jelly and the bottled quinces lining my shelves for quince and apple pies throughout the year.

Unfortunately, I needed to go to Queensland for a few days and upon my return found that the tree was almost bare. I went to ask the landowner if I could pick those that remained, only to be told that the house had recently been sold and many others had already picked the quinces, but I could certainly have any that remained. Closer inspection of the tree revealed that there were only a few poor and parrot-nibbled fruit, so I returned home devastated and empty handed.

This was quite a dilemma, as I'd planned to make quince jelly 2 days later in a cooking class. I remembered that an apple orchardist on our Tasman peninsula once told me quinces grew free and wild on his property, and that I could pick all I wanted. Courtney and I decided to explore this possibility. We sought directions from him at the packing sheds—we were to go to a quarry, follow a road down to where the pickers were working, and then follow the creek. 'They're a bit hard to get at,' he said, 'but there should be plenty there.' We set out with enthusiasm, promising to return with jars of quince jelly as a token of our appreciation in a few days.

When we arrived at the orchards in the late afternoon, there was truly nothing more beautiful; it is one of those places where time seems to stand still. There were rows of apple and pear trees as far as the eye could see. Underneath the trees was a veritable paradise—sunlight dappled through the leaves and lush green grass brush against our ankles, refreshingly damp with the afternoon dew. The sweet scent of apples and pears hung in the air. I'd never been in the orchards before—a sideward glance driving past in the hustle and bustle of daily life had given no indication of how beautiful they actually are. Woofers— backpackers from around the world who fund their travels by seasonal fruit picking—worked alongside local pickers, all of them happy, tanned and healthy from the sunny days in the orchard.

As idyllic as the setting was, we could not see any creek. A local picker came to the rescue. 'How can I help you ladies?' he asked. We told him of our quince mission, which immediately sparked an enthusiastic conversation among the bystanders. 'Oh, I remember quince jelly,' one Englishman said. 'There's nothing quite like it. Haven't tasted it in years! My mum used to make it.' Much to his delight we told him of our promise to deliver many jars within a few days to the packing sheds.

The elderly picker took the time to walk us through the orchards and down to the creek, and there were the quince trees—about 15 in all. He left us to it, after showing us the way to cross the creek without sinking waist deep in water, and pressing a freshly picked pear into each of our hands to eat along the way. We were able to get to a few, but it seemed that the parrots or other quince seekers had been there before us, so we left with a mere half dozen.

What were we to do? We had barely enough to make 3 jars. How would we keep our promise to the pickers and orchardist for their jars of jelly? How were we to make our toffee quinces? As sometimes happens, things have a way of working out. While we were driving home my daughter Stephanie rang, ecstatic because she had found near her new home in the Derwent Valley a quince tree dropping its unwanted fruit onto the ground. She was about to take her clothes' baskets to pick the lot, and she did—enough for all she needed and plenty for me besides.

Then, when we arrived home, there was a message on our answering machine from a total stranger who had an abundance of quinces: we could have half a wheelbarrowful. 'Did we want them?' he asked. Did we ever! Arrangements were made to pick these up within a few days, and Stephanie and her family arrived to deliver her pickings to us.

So everything came together in the end. And as I write this, there is quince jelly once more lining the benches and more on the stove. Friends will be contacted to come to indulge in toffee quinces once more. And, of course, the fruit pickers and orchardist will receive their share.

This luxurious abundance has enabled me to explore other recipes; quince and melon cheese is a new treat this year. A friend told me that an elderly acquaintance insisted that quince and melon jam is simply the best, so I tried this out. Quite by accident I cooked it a bit past the jam stage, so turned it into a fruit cheese to serve with camembert or brie. The flavour certainly is sensational.

From a less than promising start, the supply of quinces this year has been truly amazing. Along the way we met some wonderful people; growers, pickers and Woofers, all of them appreciative of the incredible quince and all it can do. So it is that we look forward to next autumn with even more anticipation, when we will renew the friendships from this season in our ongoing quest for quinces.

QUINCE JELLY

1.5kg (3lb 5oz) quinces
juice of 1 lemon
water
sugar

Wash the quinces to remove the furry bloom and chop into 2.5cm (1in) pieces.

Combine the quince and lemon juice in a large saucepan and add just enough water to barely cover. Bring to the boil and simmer for about 40 minutes, or until the quinces are tender.

Strain through a colander, then strain the liquid again through a sieve lined with a double thickness of muslin.

For each cup of liquid add 1 cup of sugar.

Combine the liquid and the sugar in a large saucepan over medium heat and bring to the boil, stirring occasionally to dissolve the sugar. Continue to boil, without stirring, until setting point is reached (see note).

Pour into warm sterilised jars and seal immediately. The jelly can be eaten immediately. Store in a cool, dry and dark place for up to 18 months.

Makes approximately 1.75 litres (61fl oz)

Note: *To test if jelly is set, place 2 teaspoons of the mixture onto a cold saucer and place in the fridge for 5 minutes. Run your finger through the cold jelly. It has reached setting point if the surface is quite firm and wrinkles when you pull your finger through it.*

ROAST CHICKEN WITH CITRUS QUINCE JUS

3 tablespoons canola or peanut oil
2 x 1kg (2lb 4oz) chickens
½ cup **quince jelly**
juice of 1 lemon
½ teaspoon salt
½ cup orange juice

QUINCE JUS
1 cup water
1 teaspoon chicken or vegetable stock powder
1 teaspoon tomato paste
1 teaspoon **tomato sauce**
3 teaspoons cornflour mixed to a paste with a
    little cold water

Preheat the oven to 180°C (350°F/gas 4).

Pour the oil into roasting tin and place in the oven for 10 minutes. Roll the chickens in the hot oil and turn to breast side up.

Place the quince jelly, lemon juice, salt and orange juice in a small saucepan. Bring to the boil, simmer until the quince jelly has melted and pour half over the chickens. Roast for 30 minutes, basting after 15 minutes. Remove from the oven, pour on the remaining quince sauce and roast, basting every 15 minutes, for 30 minutes or until the chickens are cooked. Transfer the chickens to a large plate, cover loosely with foil and set aside in a warm place.

For the quince jus, pour the fat from the pan and discard. Add the water, stock powder, tomato paste and tomato sauce to the roasting tin and bring to the boil over medium heat, stirring. Strain if desired. Add some or all of the cornflour paste and stir until thickened. Season to taste with salt and pepper.

Carve each chicken into quarters. Place a little of the quince jus on each plate and place a portion of chicken on top. Drizzle the remaining jus over the chicken and serve with roast potatoes, pumpkin, parsnips and steamed seasonal vegetables.

Serves 4–6

CITRUS CHICKEN

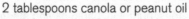

2 tablespoons canola or peanut oil
4 skinless chicken breast fillets
¼ cup dry white wine
juice of 1 small lemon
juice of 1 orange
2 teaspoons finely grated lemon zest
2 teaspoons finely grated orange zest
3 teaspoons **quince jelly**
2 teaspoons chicken stock powder
1 teaspoon **tomato chutney** (or any sort)
¾ cup pouring cream
3 teaspoons cornflour mixed to a paste with a little
    cold water
½ cup freshly grated tasty cheese

Preheat the oven to 180°C (350°F/gas 4). Grease a 1.5-litre (52fl oz)
baking dish.

Heat the oil in a large frying pan over medium–high heat. Add the chicken
breasts and cook on each side until lightly browned and almost cooked
through. Remove the chicken from the pan and transfer to the prepared dish.

Add the wine, lemon and orange juices and zests, quince jelly, stock powder,
tomato chutney and cream to the pan and place over medium heat. Bring to
the boil, add some or all of the cornflour paste and whisk until thickened. Pour
over the chicken and scatter on the cheese. Bake for 15 minutes or until the
cheese is golden and melted. Serve with fresh seasonal vegetables.

Serves 4

FELTIES

These small fruit tarts were named originally by our children as 'fat lady tarts', which they later shortened to Felties.

  1 x quantity **sweet shortcrust pastry**
  125g (4½oz) dark cooking chocolate, chopped
  125g (4½oz) cream cheese, softened
  2 tablespoons icing sugar
  2 teaspoons lemon juice
  250g (9oz) strawberries, hulled and halved
  ¾ cup **quince jelly**, melted

Preheat the oven to 180°C (350°F/gas 4). Grease 24 patty pan holes.

Roll out the pastry on a lightly floured bench to 3mm (⅛in) thick and cut into rounds to fit the patty pan holes. Line the pans with the pastry rounds, prick each 3 times with a fork and place in the fridge for 15 minutes.

Remove the patty pans from the fridge and bake the pastry in the oven for 8–10 minutes or until lightly golden. Allow to stand in the pans for 10 minutes, then transfer onto a wire rack to cool.

Break the chocolate into small pieces and melt in a heatproof bowl over a saucepan of simmering water. Brush the inside of the tartlet cases with a thin layer of melted chocolate and allow to set.

Combine the cream cheese, icing sugar and lemon juice in a bowl and mix until smooth. Spoon into tartlets.

Arrange the strawberries on top of each tartlet. Brush with a little quince jelly to glaze. Transfer to the fridge for 30 minutes or until set.

Makes 24

PAPRIKA CHICKEN WITH QUINCE JUS

The spice mixture in this recipe is the best ever. I quadruple the quantities and store the excess in a jar. It keeps for 6 months.

1 tablespoon paprika
¾ tablespoon sugar
½ tablespoon salt
¼ tablespoon ground black pepper
¼ cup peanut oil
1kg (2lb 4oz) chicken breast fillets

QUINCE JUS
¼ cup dry white wine
2 teaspoons **quince jelly**
2 teaspoons tomato paste
1½ cups chicken stock
3 teaspoon cornflour mixed to a paste with a little cold water

Preheat the oven to 200°C (400°F/gas 6).

Combine the paprika, sugar, salt and pepper in a small bowl and mix well. Pour the oil into a roasting tin. Add the chicken fillets, sprinkle liberally with half the spice mixture, then turn and sprinkle on the remaining spice mixture. Roast for 5 minutes. Reduce the oven temperature to 170°C (325°F/gas 3) and cook, basting in pan juices after 10 minutes, for 15–20 minutes or until cooked through. Remove the chicken from the tin and keep hot.

For the quince jus, pour off any fat from the tin. Place the tin over low heat and add the wine, quince jelly, tomato paste and stock, stirring. Bring to the boil and add some or all of the cornflour paste, stirring until thickened.

Serves 4–6

Rum Balls

200g (7 oz) dark cooking chocolate, chopped
400g (14oz) left-over cake (such as plain, chocolate or
    fruit), crumbed finely
3 teaspoons **quince jelly**
¼ cup rum
1 cup desiccated coconut

Break the chocolate into small pieces and melt in a heatproof bowl over a saucepan of simmering water.

Mix the cake crumbs and quince jelly into the chocolate together with the rum. Allow to stand for 10 minutes or until the mixture is firm enough to roll into balls. Shape into walnut-sized balls and roll in the coconut. Leave to set for at least 1 hour before serving.

Store in an airtight container for up to 7 days. In warmer climates, store in the fridge.

Makes approximately 24

Hint: *Freeze left-over portions of cake until you have enough for a batch of these rum balls. Biscuit crumbs can also be used, but they tend to make the rum balls a little gritty and dry.*

SLOW-ROASTED LAMB WITH QUINCE JUS

3 tablespoons light olive oil or canola oil
2kg (4lb 8oz) boned leg of lamb or loin roast
¼ cup **quince jelly**
½ cup apple juice
¼ cup water

QUINCE JUS
1½ cups chicken stock
2 teaspoons chutney (any sort)
3 teaspoons cornflour mixed to a paste with
    ¼ cup cold water

Preheat the oven to 180°C (350°F/gas 4). Pour the oil into a roasting tin
and place in the oven for 10 minutes. Remove from the oven and roll the
lamb in the hot oil. Spoon the quince jelly over the lamb and pour the apple
juice and water into the base of the tin.

Return to the oven and reduce the temperature to 160°C (315°F/gas 2–3).
Cook, basting with the pan juices every 30 minutes, for approximately
1½ hours or until the lamb is tender. Remove the lamb and place on a
platter. Cover loosely with foil and set aside in a warm place for 15 minutes.

For the quince jus, pour any excess fat from the tin and discard. Place tin over
medium heat. Add the stock and chutney and bring to the boil, stirring. (If jus
needs more flavour, add a little tomato, soy and/or Worcestershire sauce.)
Strain the liquid through a sieve if you'd like a smooth jus. Return the liquid to
the tin, add some or all of the cornflour paste and stir until thickened. Season.

Slice the lamb and place on serving plates. Drizzle with a little of the quince
jus and serve with roasted or steamed seasonal vegetables.

Serves 6

RASPBERRIES

RASPBERRY JAM

1.5kg (3lb 5oz) raspberries
¼ cup water
juice of 1 lemon
1.5kg (3lb 5oz) sugar

Place the raspberries, water and lemon juice in a saucepan over medium heat and bring to the boil. Reduce heat to low and simmer for 5 minutes. Add the sugar and return to the boil, stirring until the sugar has dissolved. Boil quite briskly without stirring, for 10 minutes. Stand for 5 minutes, then pour into warm sterilised jars and seal.

Store in a cool, dry and dark place for up to 12 months.

Makes 2kg (4lb 8oz)

Hint: *Raspberry jam keeps its flavour well when stored in its jar in the freezer. The jam never actually freezes due to its sugar content, so is still spreadable when taken out of the freezer.*

FAIL-PROOF SCONES

3 cups self-raising flour

1 heaped teaspoon baking powder

1 teaspoon icing sugar

¼ teaspoon salt

1 cup pouring or thickened cream

½ cup skim milk

½ cup water

2 tablespoons milk, for glazing

raspberry jam, to serve

crème chantilly, to serve

Preheat the oven to 190°C (375°F/gas 5). Line an 18 x 28cm (3¼ x 11¼ in) slice tin with baking paper.

Place the flour, baking powder, icing sugar and salt in a bowl and stir well. Add together the cream, skim milk and water, and mix with a metal spoon until a soft dough forms. Turn dough out onto a lightly floured bench and shape into a 2cm (¾in) thick rectangle. Dip a scone cutter in flour, cut out dough and place in tin. Glaze the tops with milk and bake for 20 minutes, or until well risen and golden.

To serve, split each scone in half, spread with raspberry jam and top with a spoonful of crème chantilly.

Makes 12

Note: *To keep scones soft when serving, remove from oven and place immediately in a large bowl lined with a tea towel and cover loosely to cool. For scones with a crisper crust when served, transfer onto a wire rack to cool.*

VARIATION

For fruit scones, add 1 teaspoon cinnamon and ½ cup sultanas or ½ cup chopped pitted dates to the scone mixture.

Raspberry Shortcake

125g (4½oz) butter, softened

125g (4½oz) sugar

1 egg

125g (4½oz) plain flour

125g (4½oz) self-raising flour

1 teaspoon finely grated lemon zest

a little egg white

¾ cup **raspberry jam**

Topping

3 egg whites

125g (4½oz) caster sugar

100g (3½oz) desiccated coconut

Preheat the oven to 170°C (325°F/gas 3). Grease a 25 x 30cm (10 x 12in) Swiss roll tin.

Whisk the butter and the sugar. Add the egg and whisk until well combined. Fold in the combined flours and lemon zest using a metal spoon to form a soft dough. Press the dough evenly into the greased tin and brush with a little egg white. Spread over the raspberry jam.

For the topping, beat the egg whites in a medium bowl until soft peaks form. Add the sugar and beat until soft peaks form again. Fold in the coconut. Place spoonfuls of the mixture over the jam, then spread out so the jam is covered completely. Bake for 30 minutes, or until the topping is light golden brown.

Serves 12

Raspberry Cream Sponge

If my maternal grandmother had a trademark recipe, then this would be it. Each Saturday I'd catch the bus and tram to her house at Sandy Bay and without fail the aroma of this cake filled the house. She baked it in a slab tin, and then after cooking cut it in half and filled it with an ample layer of raspberry cream before dusting the top with icing sugar.

I still make it to this day. I'm sure it's not as good as hers, but it's always popular. Unlike my nan, I sometimes mix about ¾ cup fresh raspberries through the cream as well. This is her time-honoured recipe.

2 large eggs
½ cup caster sugar
¾ cup self-raising flour
2 large teaspoons cornflour
1 dessertspoon softened butter melted in 2 tablespoons
    boiling milk

Raspberry cream
2 cups thickened cream
½ cup **raspberry jam**
1 tablespoon icing sugar, for dusting

Preheat the oven to 180°C (350°F/gas 4). Grease an 18 x 28 x 5cm (7 x 11¼ x 2in) deep slab tin. Line the base with baking paper and then grease the baking paper.

Beat the eggs and sugar in a large bowl until pale and thick. Fold in the sifted flour and cornflour. Drizzle the combined butter and milk down the inside of the bowl and fold in using a knife or metal spoon.

Pour the mixture into the prepared tin. Bake for 20 minutes or until a skewer inserted into the centre of the cake comes out clean. Leave to stand in the tin for 2 minutes, then turn out onto a wire rack. Leave to cool completely.

For the raspberry cream, beat the cream until soft peaks form. Add the raspberry jam and whip until thick. You may like to taste the cream after adding ¼ cup of the jam.

Cut the cake in half vertically. Spread one half with a layer of raspberry cream, then cover with the other half. Dust with icing sugar.

Serves 12

GERMAN SPICE BISCUITS

60g (2¼oz/¼ cup) butter
¾ cup golden syrup
1¾ cups plain flour
1 teaspoon mixed spice
2 teaspoons ground cinnamon
½ cup **raspberry jam**, firmly set
250g (9oz) dark chocolate, chopped
60g (2¼oz) white chocolate, chopped (optional)

Heat the butter and golden syrup in a saucepan over medium heat and bring just to the boil. Remove from heat and set aside to cool for 5 minutes. Add the flour, mixed spice and cinnamon and mix to form a soft dough. Allow to stand for 2 hours in a cool place. (For a quicker process, place mixture in fridge for 30 minutes and stir every 10 minutes until it is a good handling consistency.)

Preheat the oven to 160°C (315°F/gas 2–3). Line two baking trays with baking paper.

Turn dough out onto a lightly floured bench and knead very briefly. Roll out to 8mm (⅜in) thick and cut into 5cm (2in) rounds. Make an indentation into the centre of each round, taking care not to press all the way through. Fill indent with jam and bake for 10 minutes or until just firm. Allow to cool on the trays.

Break dark chocolate into small pieces and melt in a heatproof bowl over a saucepan of simmering water. Spread the non-jam side of each biscuit with the melted chocolate, place on a wire rack, chocolate-side up, and leave for 20 minutes or until chocolate has set. If desired, melt the white chocolate and drizzle decoratively over the dark chocolate, then place on a wire rack, chocolate side up, until set.

Makes approximately 24

STRAWBERRIES

STRAWBERRY JAM

juice of 2 lemons
¼ cup water
1.5kg (3lb 5oz) strawberries, hulled and roughly chopped
1.5kg (3lb 5oz) sugar

Combine the lemon juice, water and strawberries in a large saucepan over medium heat. Bring to the boil, stirring occasionally, and simmer for 10 minutes. Add the sugar and bring to the boil, stirring until the sugar has dissolved. Cook quite briskly without stirring for about 20 minutes until setting point is reached (see note).

Pour into warm sterilised bottles and seal. Store in a cool, dry and dark place for up to 12 months.

Makes approximately 2kg (4lb 8 oz)

Note: *To test if jam is set, place 2 teaspoons of the mixture onto a cold saucer and place in the fridge for about 5 minutes. Run your finger through the cold jam. It has reached setting point if the surface is quite firm and wrinkles when you pull your finger through it.*

CLASSIC SWISS ROLL

—•

3 eggs
½ cup caster sugar
1 cup self-raising flour, sifted
2 tablespoons hot milk
¼ cup caster sugar, extra
¾ cup **strawberry jam**
icing sugar, for dusting

Preheat the oven to 200°C (400°F/gas 6). Grease a 20 x 30cm (8 x 12in) Swiss roll tin and line with baking paper.

Beat the eggs and sugar in a medium bowl until pale and thick. Fold in the flour using a knife ormetal spoon. Drizzle the milk down the inside edge of the bowl and fold in until just combined. Pour the mixture evenly into the prepared tin. Bake for 8–10 minutes or until a skewer inserted into the centre of the cake comes out clean.

Meanwhile, place a piece of baking paper slightly larger than the tin on the bench and sprinkle with extra sugar. Working quickly, turn the still warm cake out onto the sugared paper, remove the lining paper, and roll up, using the sugared paper as a guide. Wrap in a clean tea towel and set aside to cool completely. Unroll, remove the paper and spread the inside surface with the strawberry jam. Re-roll, dust with icing sugar and cut into slices to serve.

Serves 6

CREAM HORNS

For this recipe you will need cream horn tins. These can be purchased very reasonably at kitchen supply stores and can often be found at large supermarkets. The financial outlay is well worthwhile—cream horns are simple to make and are always well received.

1 sheet frozen puff pastry, thawed
¼ cup **strawberry jam**, approximately
1 x quantity **crème chantilly**
1 punnet small strawberries
icing sugar, for dusting (optional)

Preheat the oven to 200°C (400°F/gas 6). Grease the outside of 12 cream horn tins and line a baking tray with baking paper.

Cut the pastry into 8mm (⅜in) wide strips. Wind the pastry strips around each greased horn tins and place on the prepared tray, allowing a little room for spreading. Bake for 10 minutes or until golden brown. Slide the pastry horns off the tins (if the inside is still a little moist, return to the oven for a couple of minutes to dry out). Transfer to a wire rack to cool.

About 30 minutes before serving, spoon ½ teaspoon strawberry jam into the base of each horn, then fill with the crème chantilly. Place a small strawberry in the end and dust with icing sugar, if desired.

The unfilled pastries keep well, stored in an airtight container, for 7 days.

Serves 6-8

VARIATION

Matchsticks

If you don't have cream horn tins, a good substitute is to make matchsticks.

Simply cut the pastry sheet in half, then cut each half into three or four fingers. Place side by side on a baking tray lined with baking paper and bake in a 200°C (400°F/gas 6) preheated oven for 10 minutes or until puffed and golden.

When cold, cut in half lengthways. Spread the base with **strawberry jam**, then top with a layer of **crème chantilly**. Place the top piece on the cream and dust with icing sugar.

Nanna's Little Cheesecakes

1 x quantity **sweet shortcrust pastry**
a little egg white
½ cup **strawberry jam**, approximately
1 egg
¾ cup sugar
¾ cup milk
1½ cups self-raising flour
60g (2¼oz) butter, melted
2 teaspoons finely grated lemon rind

Lemon glace icing
1½ cups icing sugar
2 teaspoons melted butter
1 tablespoon lemon juice
1 tablespoon boiling water, approximately

Preheat the oven to 180°C (350°F/gas 4). Grease 24 scoop patty pan holes.

Roll out shortcrust pastry on a lightly floured bench to 3mm (⅛in) thick. Cut into rounds to fit patty holes. Line the holes with the pastry rounds and brush with egg white. Place ½ teaspoon strawberry jam in each pastry case.

Whisk the egg and sugar in a bowl until pale and thick. Add the milk, flour, butter and lemon rind all at once and mix until smooth. Place 2 teaspoonfuls of mixture in each pastry case. Bake for 12 minutes or until the cakes are golden brown. Allow to cool in the pans for 5 minutes, then transfer to a wire rack to cool completely.

For the lemon glace icing, mix the icing sugar, butter and lemon juice. If icing is too thick, add a few drops of boiling water. Spread each tartlet with icing.

Makes approximately 24

LOBSTER MEDALLIONS WITH STRAWBERRY CHILLI GLAZE

1kg (2lb 4oz) cooked lobster
¼ cup **strawberry jam**
½ cup **sweet chilli sauce**
2 teaspoons dry white wine

Remove the legs from the lobster and set aside. Cut the lobster in half lengthways and remove the meat. Reserve the pieces from the legs for another use.

Cut the meat into 2cm (¾in) medallions and place on a serving platter.

Strain the strawberry jam and sweet chilli sauce into a small bowl, add the white wine and mix well. Drizzle over the lobster meat and serve.

Serves 2

VARIATION

This dish can also be served hot. Heat the strawberry chilli glaze before drizzling over the warm lobster medallions.

TOMATOES

Above all other fruits, tomatoes reign supreme for their usefulness in cooking. I freeze, bottle and semi-dry them, and make chutneys, pickles, jams (truly), passata, pasta and pizza sauces.

This passion for tomatoes most likely dates back to the several months I spent living with an Italian family. When I first went to board with them, I had no idea of the gastronomic delights that were part of the deal. Their way of life related forthrightly and unashamedly to all that food and cooking can be. It wasn't just about what was served on the plate, though that was cause enough for celebration, but it was far more: a sense of family and community was seemingly woven into the food.

They had weekly get-togethers for friends and family; occasions where dishes were piled high with food and crusty breads, and olive oil and pasta were everywhere, ample for everyone but visitors would bring even more. Recipes were exchanged, samplings and hints offered liberally—never in a spirit of competition, always in an appreciation for the food.

I think it was here that I finally felt that there was a licence to love to cook: for the sake of the produce and the end product, for the sake of the people; friends and family and anyone who had entered their lives at the time, such as the likes of me.

They were so generous in sharing their cooking secrets, and sometimes this took an interesting turn. One evening, the father of the house, Angelo, had decided to demonstrate to me his skill in slaughtering a chicken, so that it was more tasty and tender when cooked. To my horror he brought the poor bird into the kitchen and wrung its neck. I made for the bathroom so as not to witness the scene, and spent half an hour weeping for the poor creature. I couldn't eat chicken there ever again—I like my meat anonymous even to this day. He could have taken this as a tremendous insult I know, but with characteristic good humour he merely used to tease me about it.

When grapes were in season, he would arrive home from his work as a builder with his ute loaded with boxes of grapes that he'd haggled for at the market. From these he made his own table wine for meals, a lovely fruity scarlet brew that he used to prepare in two old concrete laundry tubs out the back. He crushed the grapes by hand himself (or let the children stomp them), then bottled it. It was a little like a lambrusco, but this is probably an insult to his brewing expertise.

In the back shed, he also made, by some mysterious process, a fiery spirit that he and his friends drank neat. He was immensely proud of it. One night for my benefit and admiration, he poured a small pool of it onto their laminex kitchen table and set it alight. 'See how good it is!' he enthused. 'See how it burns with a purple flame! It is 97 per cent proof.' I didn't have cause to doubt it. When once I tasted a small sip at his insistence my throat was sore for days afterwards.

When I think back on those times—about the fun surrounding food, the laughter, the good-natured teasing and the spirit of hospitality—I feel so privileged to have been part of their world for even such a short time.

BOTTLED TOMATOES

1kg (2lb 4oz) tomatoes, cored and chopped
½ teaspoon citric acid
tomato juice (optional)

Place the sealing rings on clean preserving jars. Add the tomatoes, filling within 1cm (½in) of rim of jars, pressing down firmly. Add the citric acid and fill to the brim with tomato juice or water. Place the lids on the jars and secure with the clips, or if using screw-top jars, screw lids on.

Place the jars in the preserving outfit. Fill preserver with cool water to just cover the lids of the jars. Bring to 100°C (212°F), making sure that this takes at least 1 hour. Hold at this temperature for 30 minutes for bottles containing up to 10 cups of product. Add an extra 10 minutes for larger bottles.

Alternatively, place the jars in a large saucepan in which a rack has been placed at the base—the jars should not touch each other (you can place a little folded newspaper between them). Bring slowly to the boil (this should take at least an hour). Boil steadily for 25 minutes. Turn off the heat and allow to stand in the pan for 1 hour.

Remove jars from preserver or pan and place on a chopping board. Leave to stand for 48 hours. Remove the clips, if necessary, and check that the lids are concave. Store in a cool, dark and dry place for to 18 months.

Makes 1kg (2lb 4oz)

Note: *This recipe can be made in proportion to the number of tomatoes you have on hand.*

Minestrone

1 tablespoon olive oil
125g (4½oz) bacon, rind removed and diced
1 onion, peeled and finely chopped
4 garlic cloves, peeled and crushed
1 carrot, peeled and diced
1 small potato, peeled and diced
1 red capsicum, deseeded and diced
125g (4½oz) green beans, cut into short lengths (optional)
4 rounded tablespoons tomato paste
½ teaspoon sugar
1 teaspoon dried thyme
500g (1lb 2oz) **bottled tomatoes**, drained and finely
    chopped
3 cups chicken or vegetable stock
2 cups cooked macaroni
½–¾ cup freshly grated or shaved parmesan cheese
2 tablespoons chopped parsley (optional)

Heat the oil in a large saucepan over medium heat. Add the bacon and cook for 5 minutes or until bacon begins to crisp. Stir in the onion, garlic, carrot, potato, capsicum and beans and sauté, stirring occasionally, for 5 minutes or until the onion is transparent. Add the tomato paste, sugar, thyme, bottled tomatoes and stock. Bring to the boil and simmer for 30 minutes. Add the macaroni and bring back to a simmer. Season with salt and pepper to taste. Serve the minestrone topped with the parmesan and parsley, if using.

Serves 4

PEPERONATA

2 tablespoons olive oil

1 onion, peeled and finely chopped

3 red capsicums, deseeded and chopped

4 garlic cloves, peeled and crushed

500g (1lb 2oz) tinned or **bottled tomatoes**

2 heaped tablespoons tomato paste

1 tablespoon **sweet chilli sauce**

1 dessertspoon soy sauce

1 dessertspoon Worcestershire sauce

1 tablespoon **tomato chutney**

3 teaspoons vegetable stock powder

1 cup water

Heat the oil in a saucepan over medium heat. Add the onion and capsicum and sauté for 5 minutes or until the onion is transparent. Stir in the garlic and cook for 1 minute. Add the remaining ingredients and bring to the boil. Cook, stirring occasionally for 30 minutes or until thick.

Serves 4

VARIATIONS

This makes a great vegetarian dish when served with pasta. Chopped zucchini and/or mushroom—about 1 cup of each—can also be added.

Sloppy Joes

The children used to love these, made from left-over peperonata.

Split hamburger rolls in half and spread with a generous amount of peperonata. Sprinkle with grated cheese and bake in the oven at 180°C (350°F/Gas 4) for 10–15 minutes or until heated through. Excellent served with a bowl of hot soup in winter, but more than acceptable at any time.

TOMATO CHILLI CHICKEN

1 tablespoon peanut oil

500g (1lb 2oz) skinless chicken breast or thigh fillets,
    sliced into strips

125g (4½oz) lean rindless bacon, diced

1 red capsicum, deseeded and diced

1 long red chilli, finely diced

1 onion, peeled and finely chopped

2 cups drained and chopped tinned or **bottled tomatoes**

3 tablespoons tomato paste

1 dessertspoon soy sauce

1 dessertspoon Worcestershire sauce

½ teaspoon sugar

1 tablespoon **sweet chilli sauce**

4 teaspoons **tomato chutney** (or any sort)

Heat the oil in a wok over medium–high heat. Add the chicken and cook
for 4 minutes or until it begins to colour. Add the bacon, capsicum, chilli
and onion and sauté, stirring occasionally, for 5 minutes or until onion is
transparent. Stir in the remaining ingredients and bring to the boil. Simmer
for 20 minutes or until the sauce is reduced and chicken is cooked through.
Add salt and pepper to taste. Serve with steamed rice, couscous or pilaf.

Serves 4

Vegetarian Pasta Sauce

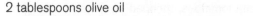

2 tablespoons olive oil

1 large onion, peeled and finely chopped

1 garlic clove, peeled and crushed

1 teaspoon ground dried basil

1 teaspoon ground dried oregano

1 tablespoon dry white wine

2 tablespoons tomato paste

½ teaspoon sugar

2 cups drained and crushed **bottled tomatoes**

½ cup freshly grated or shaved parmesan or tasty cheese

Heat the oil in a saucepan over a medium heat. Add the onion and sauté for 5 minutes or until transparent. Stir in the garlic and cook for 1 minute. Add the herbs, wine, tomato paste, sugar and bottled tomatoes. Add salt and pepper to taste. Simmer until reduced to the desired consistency.

Serve with cooked pasta and top with the cheese.

Serves 4

VARIATIONS

Marinara sauce

Add approximately 500g (1lb 2oz) of any cooked seafood of your choice to the vegetarian pasta sauce. Serve with fettuccine.

Meatballs in tomato sauce

Place freshly cooked spaghetti or fettuccine in serving bowls, top with meatballs (see page 142 for recipe), then pour on vegetarian pasta sauce and sprinkle with freshly grated parmesan cheese.

GREEN TOMATO PICKLE

3kg (6lb 12oz) green tomatoes, chopped
1kg (2lb 4 oz) onions, peeled and finely chopped
3 tablespoons cooking salt
3 cups white or cider vinegar
½ teaspoon black pepper
1kg (2lb 4oz) sugar
⅔ cup white or cider vinegar, approximately, extra
3 scant tablespoons curry powder
3 scant tablespoons mustard powder

Combine the tomato and onion in a large bowl, sprinkle on the salt and mix well. Cover and leave to stand overnight.

Next day, drain off the liquid. Place the tomato and onion in a large saucepan, add the 3 cups of vinegar, pepper and sugar and bring to the boil. Cook, stirring often, for 1 hour.

Mix extra vinegar with the curry and mustard powders to make a paste and stir into the green tomato and onion mixture. Bring to the boil and simmer for 5 minutes or until thickened and well combined. Pour into sterilised jars and seal immediately.

Eat straightaway or store in a cool, dark and dry place for up to 2 years. Serve with cold meats or cheese. It also makes a tasty addition to casserole-style dishes—they are just not the same without it.

Makes approximately 4 litres (140fl oz)

VARIATION

Green tomatoes can be sliced and dipped in flour, whisked egg and breadcrumbs and shallow fried. Drain on paper towel and serve with a little of this green tomato pickle.

Beef and Mushroom Pot Pies

1 tablespoon canola or peanut oil

500g (1lb 2oz) lean diced beef

1 onion, peeled and finely chopped

500g (1lb 2oz) mushrooms, sliced

1 heaped tablespoon **green tomato pickle**

2 teaspoons soy sauce

2 teaspoons Worcestershire sauce

1 teaspoon salt

1 cup water

3 teaspoons cornflour mixed to a paste with a little cold water.

1 sheet frozen puff pastry, thawed, or **shortcrust pastry**

Heat the oil in a large saucepan over medium–high heat. Add the beef and onion and sauté for 5 minutes or until the beef is well coloured. Stir in the mushrooms and sauté for a further 4 minutes. Add the pickle, soy and Worcestershire sauces, salt and water and bring to the boil. Reduce the heat to low and simmer for 1½ hours or until the beef is tender. Add some or all of the cornflour paste and stir until thickened. Add salt and pepper to taste.

Preheat the oven to 200°C (400°F/gas 6) and have at hand four 1½-cup ramekins or pie dishes.

Divide the mixture between the ramekins or dishes. Dampen the rim of each ramekin or dish with a little water.

Cut out rounds from the pastry and cover the ramekins or dishes. Press around the edges to seal. Bake for 10 minutes or until the pastry is puffed and golden.

Serves 4

CREAMY SEAFOOD VOL-AU-VENTS

———o———

This recipe is suited to almost any type of fish. Cooked crayfish is also particularly good; scallops and mussels are excellent.

500g (1lb 2oz) fish fillets, such as ling or flathead

6 large vol-au-vent cases

90g (3¼oz) butter

1 onion, peeled and finely chopped

5 tablespoons plain flour

3 cups milk

3 teaspoons **green tomato pickle**

1 cup freshly grated tasty cheese, plus ½–1 cup extra

1 cup frozen peas (optional)

1 cup frozen corn (optional)

Steam the fish until *just* cooked, then cut into 1cm (½in) pieces.

Preheat the oven to 200°C (400°F/gas 6). Line 2 baking trays with baking paper and place vol-au-vent cases on top.

Melt the butter in a large saucepan over medium heat. Add the onion and sauté for 5 minutes or until transparent. Stir in the flour and cook for 1 minute, stirring. Gradually whisk in the milk, stirring constantly. Bring to the boil, still stirring, and simmer for 3 minutes or until thickened. Add the green tomato pickle and cheese, and peas and corn, if using. Add salt and pepper to taste. Carefully mix in the cooked fish.

Fill the vol-au-vent cases with the seafood mixture and sprinkle on the extra cheese. Bake for 10–15 minutes or until the cheese is melted and golden.

Serves 6

VARIATIONS

For a really economical meal, substitute the fresh fish with a 425g (15oz) tin of tuna or salmon, drained.

If using scallops, clean and cover with boiling water. Leave to stand for 5 minutes, then drain and use in the recipe.

Seafood casserole

Instead of filling vol-au-vent cases, pour into a casserole or lasagne dish and sprinkle with crushed cornflakes, dot with butter and bake in the oven at 170°C (325°F/gas 3) for 20 minutes. Alternatively, top with **curried breadcrumbs.**

Curried Scallops

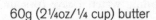

60g (2¼oz/¼ cup) butter
2 teaspoons curry powder or **curry paste**
2 teaspoons chicken stock powder
2 rounded tablespoons plain flour
2 cups milk
2 teaspoons **green tomato pickle**, mashed until smooth
¾ cup freshly grated tasty cheese
375g (13oz) scallops, cleaned and washed

Melt the butter in a large saucepan over low heat. Add the curry and stock powder and stir for 2 minutes. Then add the flour and cook for 2 minutes, stirring constantly. Gradually whisk in the milk, increase to medium heat and bring to the boil, stirring constantly. Reduce heat and simmer, stirring, for 3 minutes. Mix in the green tomato pickle and cheese and bring just to boiling point.

Place scallops in a bowl and pour over boiling water. Leave to stand for 5 minutes and then drain well. Add the scallops to the prepared sauce and barely simmer for 2 minutes or until scallops are just cooked through. Add salt and pepper to taste.

Serves 4

VARIATION

This mixture makes a very good filling for scallop pies. Cooked crayfish meat from a 1kg (2lb 4oz) crayfish can also be used in place of the scallops.

SAUSAGE ROLLS

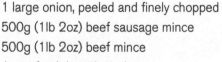

1 large onion, peeled and finely chopped
500g (1lb 2oz) beef sausage mince
500g (1lb 2oz) beef mince
1 cup fresh breadcrumbs
1 tablespoon **green tomato pickle**
1 tablespoon soy sauce
1 tablespoon Worcestershire sauce
1 teaspoon salt
2 sheets frozen puff pastry, thawed

Preheat the oven to 200°C (400°F/gas 6). Line 2 baking trays with baking paper.

Combine the onion, sausage and beef mince, breadcrumbs, green tomato pickle, soy and Worcestershire sauces and salt in a large bowl and mix until well combined.

Cut each sheet of pastry in half. Brush down one long edge of each piece with water.

Divide the mince mixture into four equal portions. Form one portion into a long sausage shape and place in the centre of a pastry sheet. Brush one edge of the pastry with water. Roll up and cut into 5 or 6 pieces. Repeat with the remaining mince mixture and pastry.

Prick each sausage roll twice with a fork. Place on the prepared trays and bake for 15 minutes or until the pastry is puffed and golden and the meat cooked through.

Makes 20–24

PASSATA

—○

1.5kg (3lb 5oz) ripe tomatoes
2 teaspoons sugar
1 teaspoon salt (optional)
¾ teaspoon citric acid, approximately

Remove the stalk end and the tough surrounding flesh on the tomatoes. Place the tomatoes, sugar and salt, if using, in a saucepan over medium–high heat. Bring to the boil and simmer until reduced to two-thirds the original volume. Strain into freezer containers, allowing headspace for expansion. Seal and once cooled, place in the freezer.

Alternatively, to bottle the passata, place the sealing rings on clean preserving jars. Do not be tempted to add onions, garlic or herbs to the passata. Fill the preserving jars to almost full. Fill the jar or bottle to the brim with a little water or tomato juice. Place the lids on the jars and secure with the clips, or if using screw-top jars, screw the lids on. Place the jars in the preserver and fill with cool water to barely cover the lids of the jars. Bring to 100°C (212°F)—this should take at least 1 hour—and hold at this temperature for 25 minutes. (For screw lid jars, tighten lids at this point.) For bottles containing over 10 cups of product allow an extra 10 minutes. (See Variation for alternative preserving method.)

Turn off the preserver and leave jars to stand for 1 hour. Remove the jars and place on a chopping board for 48 hours. Remove the clips, if used, and check that the lids are concave. Store in a cool, dry and dark place for up to 12 months.

Makes approximately 1kg (2lb 4oz)

Note: *Recipe can be made in proportion to the number of tomatoes you have on hand.*

VARIATION

Preserving passata

If you do not have a preserving outfit, you can preserve passata in a large pot on the stovetop. You will need a wire rack which fits in the bottom of the pot.

Place the filled bottles on the rack. To make sure that the bottles do not touch each other during the preserving process, insert a little folded newspaper between the bottles.

Fill the pot with cool water to cover the lids, then cover the pot with the lid and bring to the boil—make sure it takes at least 1 hour to do this. Boil for 25 minutes. (Allow 30 minutes for boiling if jars contain more than 10 cups of product.) Turn off the heat and allow the bottles to stand for 1¼ hours before removing from the pot.

RICOTTA AND SPINACH CANNELLONI BAKE

500g (1lb 2oz) ricotta cheese
125g (4½oz) frozen spinach, thawed and drained
1 cup freshly grated tasty cheese
½ cup shaved parmesan cheese
3 eggs, lightly beaten
250g (9oz) cannelloni tubes
1 tablespoon chopped basil leaves or ½ teaspoon dried
  basil
1 litre (35fl oz) **passata**, salted to taste
½ cup freshly grated tasty cheese, extra

Preheat the oven to 180°C (350°F/gas 4). Grease an 18 x 28cm
(7 x 11¼in) lasagne dish.

Combine the ricotta, spinach, tasty cheese, parmesan and eggs in a bowl.
Season with salt and pepper. Spoon the filling mixture into a piping bag fitted
with a 2cm (¾in) nozzle and pipe into the cannelloni tubes. Alternatively,
spoon the mixture into a zip-lock plastic bag, cut a small hole in one corner
and pipe into the cannelloni tubes.

Mix the basil into the passata and pour one-third into the base of the
prepared dish. Arrange the filled cannelloni tubes on top and pour on the
remaining passata mixture. Scatter on the extra grated cheese and bake for
30 minutes or until the cheese is golden brown and the cannelloni is tender.

Serves 6

Hint: *Fresh silverbeet or spinach can be used instead of frozen. Steam for 3 minutes,
drain well and cool, then chop finely.*

LASAGNE

MEAT SAUCE

1 tablespoon olive oil

750g (1lb 10oz) beef mince

2 onions, peeled and finely chopped

4 garlic cloves, peeled and crushed

4 heaped tablespoons tomato paste

1 tablespoon chopped fresh rosemary

2 tablespoons **tomato chutney**

3 teaspoons soy sauce

2 teaspoons Worcestershire sauce

¼ cup red wine

1 teaspoon salt

2 cups **passata**

3 teaspoons cornflour mixed to a paste with a little
    cold water

CREAMY CHEESE SAUCE

1 litre (35fl oz/4 cups) milk

3 tablespoons cornflour mixed to a paste with cold milk

1 cup freshly grated tasty cheese

1 tablespoon freshly grated or shaved parmesan cheese

pinch of ground nutmeg

1 egg, lightly beaten

250g (9oz) lasagne sheets

½ cup freshly grated parmesan cheese

For the meat sauce, heat the oil in a large saucepan over medium–high heat. Add the mince and cook uncovered, stirring constantly, until browned. Add the onion and garlic and cook for 2 minutes. Add the tomato paste, rosemary, tomato chutney, soy and Worcestershire sauces, red wine, salt and passata and cook over low heat, stirring occasionally, for 30 minutes. Add a little or all of the cornflour paste and stir until thickened. Season with salt and pepper.

For the creamy cheese sauce, bring the milk to the boil in a saucepan, whisk in enough cornflour paste to thicken until a yoghurt-type consistency forms. Remove from the heat and whisk in the cheeses. Season with salt, pepper and nutmeg and whisk in the egg.

Preheat the oven to 170°C (325°F/gas 3). Grease an 18 x 25cm (7 x 10in) lasagne dish.

To assemble the lasagne, place one-third of the meat sauce in the base of the prepared dish. Add a layer of lasagne sheets, then top with another one-third of the meat sauce and one-third of the creamy cheese sauce. Follow with another layer of the lasagne sheets, meat sauce and cheese sauce. Finish with a layer of lasagne sheets and cheese sauce. Sprinkle over the grated parmesan and bake for 30 minutes or until golden brown on top. Allow to stand for at least 10 minutes before cutting into slices to serve.

Serves 6

VARIATIONS

I keep a stock of pancakes (see recipe on page 74) in the freezer to use instead of lasagne sheets. They are guaranteed to be tender and the lasagne takes much less time to cook.

For gluten-free lasagne, use gluten-free plain flour in the pancakes and be sure to use maize (not wheaten) cornflour.

Homemade Baked Beans

450g (1lb) haricot or navy beans
1 tablespoon olive oil
1 teaspoon butter
2 onions, peeled and finely chopped
1 cup water
1 tablespoon mild honey
2 teaspoons **easy mustard**
1¼ cups **passata**
3 tablespoons tomato paste
3 teaspoons stock powder

Soak the beans overnight in enough water to cover plus about 1 cup extra. You may need to add more water if the beans absorb it all.

The next day, drain and rinse the beans. Place in a large saucepan, cover with water and bring to the boil. Simmer for 1 hour or until tender. Drain.

Preheat the oven to 170°C (325°F/gas 3). Have ready a 2-litre (70fl oz) casserole dish.

Heat the oil and butter in a large saucepan over medium heat. Add the onion and sauté for 5 minutes or until transparent. Remove from the heat, add the beans, water, honey, mustard, passata, tomato paste and stock powder and mix well. Pour into the casserole dish and cover with a lid or foil. Bake for 20 minutes, remove from oven, stir, replace lid or foil and bake for another 20 minutes or until the sauce has thickened. Add salt and pepper to taste.

Serves 6

SEMI-DRIED TOMATOES

—o

I always have these on hand in the fridge to use for cheese platters and pizzas.

> 2kg (4lb 8oz) ripe red tomatoes
> 1 cup white, cider or white wine vinegar, approximately
> 1½ cups light olive oil, approximately

Cut the tomatoes into eighths or quarters, depending on their size.

If you have a food dehydrator, place the segments on the trays and dehydrate on the highest setting until semi-dried (this will take approximately 6 hours).

If you are using the oven to dehydrate, preheat the oven to 70°C (150°F/gas ¼). Arrange the tomato segments in a single layer on wire racks placed on baking trays and dry for about 6 hours, or until semi-dried. Open the oven door occasionally to allow built-up moisture to escape. The tomatoes are ready when they are reduced to approximately one-third their original size.

Dip the semi-dried tomato segments into the vinegar before packing into sterilised jars. Do not pack too tightly. Pour in enough olive oil to cover, ensuring that the tomatoes are completely immersed and that there are no air bubbles.

Store semi-dried tomatoes in the fridge. If the oil solidifies, simply remove the jar from the fridge and allow to stand at room temperature for 1–2 hours before serving. The oil will liquefy once more.

Makes approximately 300g (10½oz)

Hint: *Drained of the olive oil in which they are preserved, semi-dried tomatoes make an excellent addition to pasta sauces. The oil can be used as part of a dressing for a salad or for sautéing vegetables, meat or chicken.*

Potatoes with Tomato and Olive Sauce

—◦

⅓ cup extra virgin olive oil

4 garlic cloves, peeled and crushed

1½ cups pitted kalamata olives

2 tablespoons tomato paste

¾ cup **semi-dried tomatoes,** chopped

1½ cups **passata**

750g (1lb 10oz) potatoes, peeled and cut into
    3cm (1¼in) chunks

2 teaspoons chopped fresh rosemary or basil leaves

Heat the oil in a large saucepan over medium heat. Add the garlic and
sauté for 1 minute. Stir in the olives, tomato paste, semi-dried tomatoes,
passata and potatoes and bring to the boil. Reduce heat to low and add
the rosemary or basil. Simmer for about 20 minutes or until the potatoes
are cooked through and have absorbed almost all the sauce. Add salt and
pepper to taste.

Serves 6 as a side dish, or 4 as a main dish

CHICKEN AND SEMI-DRIED TOMATO CANNELLONI

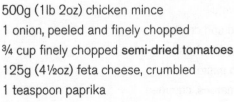

500g (1lb 2oz) chicken mince
1 onion, peeled and finely chopped
¾ cup finely chopped **semi-dried tomatoes**
125g (4½oz) feta cheese, crumbled
1 teaspoon paprika
1 packet cannelloni tubes
400g (14oz) tinned or **bottled tomatoes**
1 cup **passata**
2 teaspoons Worcestershire sauce
½–¾ cup freshly grated tasty cheese

Preheat the oven to 170°C (325°F/gas 3). Grease an 18 x 28cm
(7 x 11¼in) lasagne dish.

In a medium bowl, combine the chicken mince, onion, semi-dried tomatoes,
feta, paprika and salt and pepper to taste. Spoon the mixture into a piping
bag fitted with a 2cm nozzle or a zip-lock plastic bag with a small hole cut in
one corner and pipe into the tubes.

Mix the tomato, passata and Worcestershire sauce in a bowl. Add salt
and pepper to taste. Then spread ⅔ cup of the mixture over the base
of the prepared dish. Place filled pasta tubes side by side in dish, then
pour remaining sauce over. Sprinkle grated cheese over the top. Bake for
30 minutes or until pasta is tender and the cheese is melted and lightly
browned.

Serves 4

SPINACH, BASIL AND SEMI-DRIED TOMATO TARTS

60g (2¼oz) baby spinach leaves, finely shredded
2 tablespoons chopped fresh basil
125g (4½oz) feta cheese, crumbled
½ cup chopped **semi-dried tomatoes**
½ cup pouring cream
3 eggs, lightly beaten
2 sheets frozen puff pastry, thawed
½ cup freshly grated tasty cheese

Preheat the oven to 190°C (375°F/gas 5). Grease four 1-cup pie dishes.

Place the spinach in a small saucepan and pour over enough boiling water to cover. Set aside for 1 minute then drain well.

Combine the basil, feta, semi-dried tomatoes, spinach and cream in a medium bowl. Add the eggs and stir well. Season with salt.

Cut the pastry into rounds to fit the base of the prepared dishes. Line dishes with the pastry, spoon in the mixture and sprinkle with the cheese. Bake for 5 minutes. Reduce the oven temperature to 160°C (315°F/gas 2–3) and bake for a further 10 minutes or until the filling is set and the cheese is golden brown.

Serves 4

Note: *This mixture can be used without the pastry to make mini frittatas. In this case, make sure you grease the pie tins well.*

OLIVE, FETA AND SEMI-DRIED TOMATO BREAD

3 x quantities **basic bread dough**
1 cup pitted kalamata olives, halved
1 cup roughly chopped **semi-dried tomatoes**
1 cup chopped feta cheese
½ cup freshly grated tasty cheese

At the final kneading stage of the basic bread dough recipe, mix in the olives, semi-dried tomato and feta. Do not overmix at this stage, just knead briefly and form into an oval shape.

Preheat the oven to 200°C (400°F/gas 6). Line a baking tray with baking paper.

Place the bread dough on the lined tray and set aside to rise in a warm place for 20 minutes. Cut 6mm (¼in) deep slashes at 1cm (½in) intervals in the top of the dough with a serrated knife. Sprinkle over the grated cheese. Bake for 10 minutes. Reduce the oven temperature to 180°C (350°F/gas 4) and bake for a further 25 minutes or until golden with a crisp crust and the loaf sounds hollow when tapped with the fingers. Cool on a wire cake cooler.

This bread is excellent served with soups such as **minestrone** (see page 228).

Makes 1 large cob loaf

Spinach and Semi-dried Tomato Rice Bake

This is a good way to use silverbeet or spinach so that it is barely recognisable to the fussy palate, young or old. It is also good for using up leftover cooked rice.

3 eggs
pinch of cayenne pepper
pinch of ground nutmeg
1 large onion, peeled and very finely chopped or grated
1½ teaspoons salt
4 cups cooked brown or white rice
1 cup grated tasty cheese
2 teaspoons Worcestershire sauce
½ teaspoon dried thyme
2 cups finely shredded silverbeet or spinach (can be fresh
     or frozen)
1 cup chopped **semi-dried tomatoes**
1 cup milk

Topping
125g (4½oz) lean rindless bacon, diced
1 tablespoon butter, melted
½ cup freshly grated tasty cheese, extra (optional)

Preheat the oven to 170°C (325°F/gas 3). Grease a 20cm (8in) casserole dish.

Lightly whisk the eggs in a large bowl. Add the cayenne, nutmeg, onion, salt, rice, cheese, Worcestershire sauce, thyme, silverbeet or spinach, semi-dried tomatoes and milk and mix well.

Pour the egg mixture into the prepared dish and top with the bacon. Drizzle over the melted butter and top with the extra cheese, if using. Bake for 30 minutes or until set.

Serves 4

VARIATION

For a meat-free option, sliced tomatoes, sprinkled with a little salt and sugar, can be used in place of the bacon in the topping.

TOMATO CHUTNEY

Last December we received an order for 360 jars of assorted jams, pickles and chutneys for gift packs. We decided one product to include would be this tasty tomato chutney. At the end of the day we had a few excess kilos of tomatoes. I thought this presented a good opportunity to show Matthew, Courtney's boyfriend and new conscript to our kitchen, how to make this on his own. Knowing that he hated chopping apples and onions, I suggested he just prepared the rest of the ingredients and I would add those later when I had the time to attend to it.

When the time came for bottling the chutney, I realised that I never did quite get to doing them. Too exhausted to be bothered by now, we decided to puree the mixture in the food processor and call it a sauce. It turned out to be very tasty indeed and was subsequently deemed to be a new recipe named Matt's tomato sauce. It's particularly good for those whose digestive systems are sensitive to onions, or for people who simply don't like them.

2kg (4lb 8oz) tomatoes, chopped

4 small onions, peeled and finely chopped

2 cooking apples, peeled, cored and finely chopped

2 garlic cloves, peeled and crushed

2 tablespoons salt

3 teaspoons mustard powder

3 teaspoons curry powder

500g (1lb 2oz) sugar

3 cups white, cider or white wine vinegar, plus ¼ cup extra

1 tablespoon cornflour

Place the tomato, onion, apple, garlic, salt, mustard and curry powders, sugar and the 3 cups of vinegar in a large saucepan and bring to the boil over medium heat, stirring until the sugar has dissolved. Reduce heat and continue to simmer for 1½ hours, stirring occasionally.

Mix the cornflour to a paste with the extra vinegar, add some or all to the boiling mixture and stir until thickened. Pour into sterilised jars and seal immediately.

Eat at once or store in a cool, dry and dark place for up to 1 year.

Makes approximately 2kg (4lb 8oz)

MACARONI BEEF CASSEROLE

This recipe when doubled is great for feeding a crowd at short notice. It's economical to make and reheats well, and was a great standby when our children were at home and their friends came to visit.

1 tablespoon canola or peanut oil

300g (10½oz) beef mince

1 large onion, peeled and finely chopped

1 garlic clove, peeled and crushed

½ cup finely chopped red capsicum

1 teaspoon curry powder

2 heaped tablespoons tomato paste

400g (14oz) tinned or **bottled tomatoes**, crushed

1 dessertspoon soy sauce

1 dessertspoon Worcestershire sauce

2 large tablespoons **tomato chutney**

1 cup water

2 cups cooked macaroni

¾ cup freshly grated tasty cheese

Preheat the oven to 170°C (325°F/gas 3). Grease a casserole dish or 6 (1-cup capacity) ramekins.

Heat the oil in a large frying pan over medium–high heat. Add the mince and cook, stirring, until the meat changes colour and is well broken up. Add the onion, garlic and capsicum and sauté for 5 minutes or until the onion is transparent. Add the curry powder and cook for 2 minutes. Add the tomato paste, crushed tomatoes, soy and Worcestershire sauces, tomato chutney and water. Add salt and pepper to taste and bring to the boil, stirring occasionally. Mix in the macaroni. Check seasoning once more.

Pour the macaroni mixture into prepared casserole dish or individual ramekins and sprinkle the cheese over the top. Cover the dish with foil and bake for 30 minutes (20 minutes for ramekins). Remove the foil and return to the oven for 5 minutes or until the cheese is golden brown. Serve with **garlic bread** and a salad.

Serves 4–6

VARIATION

For extra nutritional value, try adding some finely chopped vegetables, such as carrot or celery, when sautéing the onion and capsicum.

PASTA CARBONARA

400g (14oz) spiralli pasta, or similar
1 tablespoon olive oil
250g (9oz) ham or lean rindless bacon, finely diced
4 garlic cloves, peeled and crushed
3 eggs
300ml (10½fl oz) thickened or pouring cream, or
    evaporated milk
3 teaspoons Dijon mustard or **mustard**
½ cup freshly grated tasty cheese
½ cup freshly grated parmesan cheese
1 tablespoon **tomato chutney**
1 tablespoon chopped parsley
½ cup freshly grated parmesan cheese, extra

Cook the pasta in boiling salted water while preparing the sauce.

Heat the oil in a large saucepan over medium heat. Add the ham or bacon and fry until crisp. Add the garlic and sauté for 1 minute.

Whisk the eggs, cream and mustard in a bowl until well combined, then pour into the bacon and garlic mixture. Cook over a very low heat, stirring constantly, until the sauce begins to thicken (do not boil). Mix in the cheeses and stir until melted, then stir in the chutney.

Stir the pasta into the carbonara sauce and heat through once more. Add salt and pepper to taste. Serve sprinkled with the parsley and extra parmesan cheese.

Serves 4

PASTIES

3 sheets frozen puff pastry, thawed, or **shortcrust pastry**
375g (13oz) beef mince
250g (9oz) potatoes, peeled and grated
1 carrot, peeled and grated (optional)
1 onion, peeled and grated
1 small swede, peeled and grated (optional)
1 small parsnip, peeled and grated (optional)
¾ teaspoon salt
30g (1oz) butter, diced
tomato chutney, to serve

Cut the puff pastry sheets into quarters. Alternatively, on a lightly floured bench or board, roll out the shortcrust pastry to 3mm (⅛in) thick and cut into 10cm (4in) diameter rounds.

Preheat the oven to 200°C (400°F/gas 6). Line two baking trays with baking paper.

Mix the mince, potato, carrot, onion, swede, parsnip and salt in a large bowl. Place 1 tablespoon of the mixture on each piece of puff pastry, slightly more if using the shortcrust pastry round). Place a piece of the butter on each.

Dampen opposite edges of each pastry piece with a little water. Fold the pastry over the meat mixture to enclose and press the edges together with a fork. Prick the top twice with a fork. Transfer to the trays and bake for 10 minutes. Reduce the oven temperature to 170°C (325°F/gas 3) and bake for a further 10 minutes or until pastry is golden brown.

To serve, split the top of each of the pasties open and place ½–1 teaspoon of tomato chutney inside.

Makes 12

Pizza

After the main part of raising our six children was coming to a close, I realised it was high time I returned to the workplace. After years of just teaching cooking as a hobby in community houses in my spare time, I knew that the moment had arrived to step over the great divide into the wider world of work.

It was extremely daunting, but I finally summoned up the courage to approach the local hotel owner and ask for a job. He told me that they were about to open a pizza kitchen and needed a kitchen hand; the job was mine if I wanted it. On the first night it took every ounce of courage I had to go to work—I was absolutely terrified.

This turned out to be one of the best jobs ever, humble though it was by most people's standards. The lady in charge of the kitchen had worked in the best pizza and pasta restaurants around Hobart for many years, and brought her accumulated knowledge to this workplace. She was fastidious about making pizzas, and took great pains to impart her knowledge to me. Out of this whole process I came to learn that the three keys to an exceptional pizza are the texture of dough, the sauce and the order of layering the toppings.

To this day pizza is one of my favourite things to cook. My husband built me a huge outdoor pizza oven, and we love to invite lots of friends around for pizza evenings. The pizzas take a mere 3–4 minutes to cook and their flavour, because of the clay-oven baking, is wonderful.

basic bread dough

SAUCE
500g (1lb 2oz) tinned or **bottled tomatoes**
2 heaped tablespoons tomato paste
2 garlic cloves, peeled and crushed
1 teaspoon sugar
½ teaspoon salt
1 tablespoon **tomato chutney**
1 rosemary sprig, leaves chopped or
    ½ teaspoon dried rosemary

TOPPINGS
meat toppings (salami, ham, pepperoni, chicken, bacon),
    thinly sliced
vegetable toppings (capsicum, tomato, olives, pineapple,
    onion, crushed garlic, herbs)
seafood (mussels, squid rings, crayfish, anchovies)
150g (5½oz) mixed mozzarella and tasty cheese per
    large pizza

Note: The amount of bread dough weight for pizzas is as
follows:
    Single—120g
    Small—300g
    Large—500g
    Family—600g

For pizza, I allow the basic bread dough to rise several times and turn it over with a spoon from time to time. When the dough is needed for the pizza, turn the dough out onto a lightly floured bench or board and knead gently. Shape the dough into balls as required and set aside in a warm place until doubled in size. If they are risen sufficiently but you are not ready to use them, simply gently press them down and reshape into a ball to rise again. This can be done several times without any ill effect on the resulting pizza.

Pat each ball out gently until it is the size you need. Place on a baking tray.

Meanwhile, for the pizza sauce, combine all the ingredients in a saucepan over medium–high heat and bring to the boil. Reduce heat to medium–low and cook, stirring occasionally, for about 20 minutes or until a thick puree has formed. Set aside to cool.

To build a pizza, there is certainly an art—or at least a method—and it truly does make all the difference. It is important not to overload the pizza with toppings, as this restricts its ability to rise. As to the amount of cheese, I was told that 150g per large- to family-sized pizza is sufficient, though I don't usually abide by this too strictly.

The pizza should be assembled as follows, always keeping to the order: bread dough; a generous spread of pizza sauce; a very thin sprinkling of freshly grated cheese; meat toppings (salami, ham, pepperoni, chicken, but not bacon at this stage); vegetable toppings; cheese; bacon; the remainder of the cheese and seafood.

Preheat the oven to 200°C (400°F/gas 6). Bake the pizza for 15–20 minutes, or until cheese is melted or crust is cooked to golden brown and crisp. If you have an outdoor pizza oven the time will generally be much reduced.

VARIATION

If you like barbecue sauce on your pizza, add approximately 1 or 2 large tablespoons of barbecue sauce to each cup of the pizza sauce.

POTATO CAKES

These potato cakes are very popular with children.

> 500g (1lb 2oz) all-purpose potatoes, peeled and
>   roughly chopped
> 1 egg
> 2 large tablespoons plain flour
> ½ teaspoon salt
> canola oil for frying
> **tomato chutney,** to serve

Combine the potatoes, egg, flour and salt in the bowl of a food processor and process until smooth.

Heat the oil in a large frying pan over medium–high. Cook tablespoonfuls of the potato mixture on each side for 2 minutes or until golden brown and crisp. Remove from the pan with an egg flip and drain on crumpled paper towel.

Serve immediately with a generous dollop of tomato chutney. They are especially good with crispy bacon, eggs and grilled tomatoes for breakfast or as a snack with a little salad on the side.

Serves 4

VARIATION

For gluten-free potato cakes, simply use gluten-free plain flour in place of regular plain flour.

SAVOURY SCROLLS

2 x quantities **basic bread dough**

FILLING

chopped ham and grated cheese mixed with a little **tomato chutney** (optional)

Follow the basic bread dough recipe and let the dough rise once. Turn the dough out onto a lightly floured bench and knead for 2 minutes or until smooth.

Preheat the oven to 190°C (375°F/gas 5). Line a baking tray with baking paper.

Shape the dough into a rectangle 1.25cm (½in) thick and spread with the filling.

Roll up, Swiss-roll style, and cut into 3cm (1¼in) slices. Place, cut side up, side by side on the lined tray. Sprinkle a little extra cheese over the top. Set aside for 15–20 minutes, or until doubled in size.

Bake the scrolls for 15–20 minutes or until well risen and golden brown.

Makes approximately 12

VARIATION

Cheese and Vegemite scrolls

Spread the basic bread dough with vegemite or similar and sprinkle on grated tasty cheese. Roll up and cut into slices, place on baking-paper lined baking trays and sprinkle with more grated cheese. Allow to rise and bake as for the savoury scrolls recipe.

MEDITERRANEAN BREADS

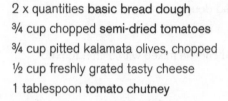

2 x quantities **basic bread dough**
¾ cup chopped **semi-dried tomatoes**
¾ cup pitted kalamata olives, chopped
½ cup freshly grated tasty cheese
1 tablespoon **tomato chutney**

Follow the basic bread dough recipe and let the dough rise once. Turn the dough out onto a lightly floured bench or board and knead for 2 minutes or until it is smooth and elastic. Divide the dough into 4 portions. Pat out into rounds about the size of a large saucer.

Combine the semi-dried tomatoes, olives, cheese and tomato chutney in a bowl. Add salt and pepper to taste. Place about 3 tablespoons of the mixture in the centre of each round of dough.

Preheat the oven to 200°C (400°F/gas 6). Line two baking trays with baking paper.

Dampen one edge of the dough, fold over and press the edges together to seal. Transfer to the lined trays, allowing room for spreading. Set aside in a warm place to rise for 15 minutes. Bake for 10 minutes. Reduce the oven temperature to 170°C (325°F/gas 3) and bake for a further 5–10 minutes or until golden brown.

Makes 4 breads

TOMATO SAUCE

6kg (13lb 8oz) tomatoes, roughly chopped
1kg (2lb 4oz) onions, peeled and chopped
750g (1lb 10oz) sugar
2 cups white wine or cider vinegar
120g (4¼oz) cooking salt
1½ tablespoons whole cloves
1½ tablespoons allspice berries
½ teaspoon cayenne pepper

Combine all the ingredients in a large saucepan and bring to the boil, then simmer, stirring regularly, for 4 hours. Strain mixture through a sieve or food mill into a clean saucepan. Bring to the boil over medium heat and then simmer for 5 minutes. Pour into warm sterilised bottles and seal immediately. Invert bottles briefly.

Store in a cool, dry and dark place for up to 2 years.

Makes approximately 7 litres (245fl oz)

Hints: *The whole spices in this recipe can be placed in muslin and tied with string to make a small bag. Remove the spice bag before straining the mixture.*

Ground spices may be used instead of whole spices. Bear in mind that these will make the sauce a little darker in colour.

CRAYFISH POT PIES

60g (2¼oz) butter
1 small onion, peeled and finely diced
2 tablespoons plain flour
2 teaspoons Dijon mustard
3 teaspoons mayonnaise
3 teaspoons **tomato sauce**
juice of ½ lemon
1½ cups milk
1 cup pouring or thickened cream
½ cup freshly grated tasty cheese
375–500g (13oz–1lb 2oz) cooked crayfish meat
1 sheet frozen puff pastry, thawed

Preheat the oven to 200°C (400°F/gas 6). Grease 4 (1-cup capacity) ramekins.

Melt the butter in a large saucepan over low heat. Add the onion and cook gently for 5 minutes. Stir in the flour and cook for 1 minute, stirring constantly. Whisk in the mustard, mayonnaise, tomato sauce, lemon juice, milk and cream and simmer, stirring constantly, for 4 minutes or until the mixture thickens. Add the cheese and stir until melted, then mix in the crayfish. Add salt and pepper to taste.

Pour crayfish mixture into ramekins. Cut 4 pieces of pastry to fit tops of ramekins and place over filling. Prick pastry twice with a fork. Place in the oven and bake for 15 minutes or until pastry is puffed and golden.

Serves 4

Honey Sesame Chicken

2 tablespoons peanut or light olive oil
750g (1lb 10oz) skinless chicken breast fillets,
    cut into strips
¼ cup honey
⅓ cup soy sauce
2 tablespoons **tomato sauce**
4 tablespoons sesame seeds

Heat the oil in a wok or large frying pan over medium heat. Add the chicken
and stir-fry for 5 minutes or until almost cooked. Pour in the honey, soy
and tomato sauces, stir to coat, and cook for 5 minutes or until the sauce
is reduced. Add the sesame seeds and cook for 3 minutes, or until a glaze
coats the chicken.

Serve with steamed rice.

Serves 4

BEEF POT ROAST

2 tablespoons plain flour

½ teaspoon salt

¼ teaspoon ground pepper

2kg (4lb 8oz) piece lean roasting beef, such as topside

2 tablespoons canola or peanut oil

1 small onion, peeled and finely chopped

2 garlic cloves, peeled and crushed

1 cup **tomato sauce** or good quality commercial
    tomato sauce

¾ cup red wine

½ teaspoon dried mixed herbs

1 cup water

3 teaspoons cornflour mixed to a paste with
    ¼ cup cold water

Combine the flour, salt and pepper in a shallow bowl. Lightly dust the beef all over in the seasoned flour.

Heat the oil in a large saucepan over medium–high heat. Add the beef and brown on all sides. Stir in the onion, garlic, tomato sauces, red wine, herbs and water. Bring to the boil, then reduce heat to low and simmer for 1½–2 hours or until the beef is very tender. Transfer to a board and leave to stand for 10 minutes before carving. Thicken the sauce if necessary by stirring in some or all of the cornflour paste. Add salt and pepper to taste. Slice meat and serve with its gravy and seasonal vegetables.

Serves 6–8

Hint: *The left-over meat is delicious, sliced and topped with* **zucchini pickle** *in sandwiches.*

Shepherd's Pie

This recipe makes good use of leftover roast lamb.

500g (1lb 2oz) lean left-over roast lamb,
    cut into 1.5cm (⅝in) pieces
1 onion, peeled and roughly chopped
1 tablespoon plain flour
¼ cup **tomato sauce**
½ teaspoon dried thyme
1½ cups milk
750g (1lb 10oz) potatoes, peeled and cubed
60g (2¼oz/¼ cup) butter
1 egg
½ teaspoon salt
½ cup freshly grated tasty cheese

Preheat the oven to 170°C (325°F/gas 3). Grease a 20cm (8in) casserole dish.

Mince the lamb and the onion, or finely chop in a food processor. Add the flour, tomato sauce, thyme, 1 cup of the milk and salt and pepper to taste. Mix well. Spoon into the casserole dish.

Meanwhile, cook the potatoes in boiling salted water until very tender. Drain and mash well. Quickly beat in the butter, egg, salt and remaining milk, mixing until very smooth. Add salt and pepper to taste. Spread over the meat and sprinkle over the cheese. Bake for 30 minutes or until cheese has melted and is lightly browned. Serve with a little extra tomato sauce.

Serves 4–6

STEAK AND STOUT

The addition of mince to this recipe gives the gravy a depth and character all its own.

  2 tablespoons canola or peanut oil
  750g (1lb 10oz) lean chuck or blade steak, cut into
      1cm (½in) cubes
  250g (9oz) good quality beef mince
  2 onions, peeled and finely chopped
  1 garlic clove, peeled and crushed
  2 cups stout
  1½ teaspoons salt
  ¼ cup **tomato sauce**
  3 teaspoons cornflour mixed to a paste with ¼ cup cold water

Heat the oil in a large saucepan over medium–high heat. Add the diced and minced beef and cook, stirring often, until browned. Stir in the onion and garlic and cook for 2 minutes. Add the stout, salt and tomato sauce and bring to the boil. Reduce the heat to low and simmer for 2 hours or until the beef cubes are tender. Thicken if necessary by stirring in some or all of the cornflour paste. Add salt and pepper to taste.

Serves 6

VARIATION

For a steak and stout pie, place a sheet of puff pastry over the meat mixture in a casserole dish. Pleat the excess pastry around the rim of the dish. Prick several times with a fork. Bake in a 200°C (400°F/gas 6) preheated oven for 20 minutes or until pastry is puffed and golden.

ZUCCHINI

ZUCCHINI PICKLE

Zucchini seems to be a vegetable that grows abundantly in home gardens. It is a pitiful waste to throw the excess away, so bags of zucchini are often seen being offered to friends, family and neighbours—in fact anyone who might remotely like them.

This zucchini pickle is one of the best preserves recipes ever. It is bright and tasty, simply delicious as an accompaniment to meats and cheeses, and elevates an ordinary sandwich from the mundane to the sublime. Our son Alistair teams this with confit duck and potato aioli as one of his delicious signature dishes.

The pickle is simplicity itself to make and takes very little time. If you make nothing else in the way of preserves, do give this a try, and also the dip that is made from it (see recipe on page 273).

> 1kg (2lb 4oz) zucchini, finely chopped
> 2 large onions, peeled and finely chopped
> 1 red capsicum, deseeded and finely chopped
> ¼ cup salt
> 2 cups sugar
> 2 cups white or cider vinegar,
>   plus 2 tablespoons extra

2 teaspoons mustard powder

2 teaspoons turmeric

2 teaspoons cornflour

Place the zucchini, onion and capsicum in a large bowl, add the salt and mix well. Leave to stand for 3 hours. Drain well.

Combine the sugar, vinegar, mustard powder and turmeric in a large saucepan over medium heat and bring to the boil, stirring until the sugar has dissolved. Add the zucchini mixture and bring back to the boil. Simmer for 25 minutes.

Mix the cornflour with the extra vinegar and use some or all of it to thicken the mixture to a pickle-like consistency. Spoon mixture into warm sterilised jars and seal. Eat immediately or store in a cool, dry and dark place for up to 1 year.

Makes 1.5 litres (52fl oz)

Duck Breast with Zucchini Pickle and Creamy Garlic Mash

For a long time cooking duck presented a challenge for me – no matter how I cooked it the end result, though tasty, was always tough; not so good when I was paying $30.00 at least for a pack of four breasts. This method was taught to me by my son Andrew when he grew tired of my complaining—it makes the duck melt-in-the-mouth tender. Duck breast should be served medium–rare.

1kg (2lb 4oz) potatoes, peeled and cut into 1.5cm pieces

1 clove garlic, peeled and crushed

30g butter

¼ cup milk

1 egg, lightly whisked

2 tablespoons vegetable oil

4 duck breast fillets, skin on

sea salt flakes

60g butter, extra

½ cup **zucchini pickle**, to serve

To make the creamy garlic mash, cook the potato in boiling salted water until tender. Drain well and mash until very smooth. Quickly mix in the garlic, butter, milk and egg and whisk until very smooth. Keep warm.

Preheat the oven to 200°C (400°F/gas 6).

Trim off the silver skin membrane from the fleshy side of the breast. Remove the small tenderloin pieces and trim the skin from the outer edges so that it matches the size of the flesh underneath. Score the skin diagonally both ways at 1cm (½in) intervals, making sure that you do not cut into the flesh below. Sprinkle the skin side lightly with sea salt flakes.

Heat the oil in a heavy based ovenproof frying pan over a high heat. Press the duck skin side down in the frying pan and cook for a few minutes until the skin is crisp and golden. Roll duck over to coat flesh side with oil, then sprinkle surface lightly with sea salt flakes and roll back over.

Place in the oven for 3 minutes, then turn the duck over and cook for another 3 minutes. Take the frying pan out of the oven and return to the stovetop on high heat. Turn breast over to skin side up, add butter and baste constantly for 2 minutes.

Remove duck from the pan and place on a wire rack, skin side up, over a plate. Leave to stand for 2 minutes before carving. Slice lengthways. Place a mound of creamy garlic mash on each plate, top with sliced duck breast and serve with a spoonful of zucchini pickle on the side.

Serves 4

CREAMY ZUCCHINI DIP

250g (9oz) cream cheese, softened, or sour cream
¾–1 cup prepared **zucchini pickle**

Combine the cream cheese and ½ cup zucchini pickle in a bowl and mix well. Gradually add more zucchini pickle to taste.

Serve with plain crackers, crusty French bread or as part of a cheese platter.

Serves 4–6

VARIATION
Try adding a little **tomato chilli chutney** to the creamy zucchini dip.

Venison with Lemon Sage Dumplings

1 tablespoon canola or peanut oil

1kg (2lb 4oz) venison, cut into 1cm (½in) pieces

1 large onion, peeled and finely chopped

1 garlic clove, peeled and crushed

1 tablespoon tomato paste

3 teaspoons soy sauce

2 teaspoons Worcestershire sauce

1 tablespoon **zucchini pickle**

1 teaspoon salt

¼ cup red wine

1½ cups beef stock or water

3 teaspoons cornflour mixed to a paste with ¼ cup cold
    water

Lemon sage dumplings

1 cup self-raising flour

¼ teaspoon salt

2 teaspoons softened butter

½ teaspoon finely grated lemon zest

3 teaspoons chopped sage or ½ teaspoon dried sage

½ cup milk

Heat the oil in a large saucepan over medium–high heat. Add the venison
and onion and sauté for 6 minutes or until the meat is well coloured. Add
the garlic and sauté for 1 minute, then stir in the tomato paste, soy and
Worcestershire sauces, zucchini pickle, salt, red wine, stock or water and
season with salt and pepper. Bring to the boil, reduce heat to low and
simmer, covered, for 1½–2 hours or until the meat is tender.

For the lemon sage dumplings, combine the flour and salt in a bowl and rub in the butter with your fingertips. Mix in the lemon zest and sage and just enough milk to make a soft dough.

When the meat is almost ready, roll walnut-sized pieces of the dough into balls and place on top of the simmering liquid.

Grease a square of baking paper large enough to cover the pan and place, greased-side down, over the saucepan. Cover with the lid and simmer for 15 minutes. Remove the lid and paper from the pan. Remove the dumplings with a slotted spoon, place in a dish and keep warm.

Thicken the gravy if necessary by stirring in some or all of the cornflour paste. Add salt and pepper to taste. Serve the venison with the dumplings and lightly steamed seasonal vegetables.

Serves 6

Chicken and Feta Turnovers

1 onion, peeled and finely chopped
500g (1lb 2oz) chicken mince
½ cup **semi-dried tomatoes**, finely chopped
6 basil leaves, finely chopped
125g (4½oz) feta cheese, crumbled
1 cup fresh breadcrumbs
1 tablespoon **sweet chilli sauce**
1 tablespoon **zucchini pickle**
1 tablespoon **tomato sauce**
½ teaspoon salt
2 sheets frozen puff pastry, thawed and cut in half

Preheat the oven to 200°C (400°F/gas 6). Line 2 baking trays with baking paper.

Combine the onion, chicken, semi-dried tomatoes, basil, feta, breadcrumbs, sweet chilli sauce, zucchini pickle, tomato sauce and salt in a large bowl and mix well. Divide into four equal portions.

Shape each portion into a long sausage shape and place in the centre of each half sheet of pastry. Spread mixture to cover half of each section of pastry, leaving a 1cm (½in) strip clear along the outer edges. Dampen one edge of the pastry with a little cold water. Fold the pastry over the filling and press the edges together with a fork to seal.

Prick with a fork in several places. Bake for 10 minutes. Reduce to 170°C (325°F/gas 3) and cook for a further 10 minutes or until golden brown.

Serves 4

ON THE SIDE

Quite aside from the recipes that include homemade preserves, there is an array of side dishes that can accompany and enhance the meals. Ranging from the healthy to the somewhat decadent, these recipes reflect the pleasurable work of a lifetime spent trying to prepare vegetables in such a way that my children would actually eat them.

Note: *Low-fat cheese and skim milk can be substituted for full-fat varieties if preferred. Low-fat cream and butter substitutes can also be used.*

APPLE AND CELERY SALAD

This is good salad to serve with chicken dishes, such as **chilli chicken and corn parcels** (see recipe on page 148).

> 3 celery stalks, finely diced
> 2 golden delicious apples, cored and finely diced
> ¼ teaspoon sugar
> juice of ½ lemon
> 3 teaspoons light oil (optional)

Place the celery, apple and sugar in a bowl and mix in the lemon juice and oil, if using. Add salt and pepper to taste.

Serves 4

BASIC COUSCOUS

1 cup couscous
1 cup boiling chicken or vegetable stock or water

Place the couscous in a heatproof bowl. Add the boiling water, stir and cover with a plate or cling film. Allow to stand for 5 minutes, then fluff up with a fork.

Serves 4

CAULIFLOWER TEMPURA

1 cup self-raising flour
¼ teaspoon bicarbonate of soda
½ teaspoon salt
cold water
½ cauliflower, cut into florets
vegetable oil (not olive oil)

Whisk together flour, bicarbonate of soda, salt and enough cold water to make a batter of coating consistency. Leave to stand while preparing the cauliflower.

Boil, steam or microwave the cauliflower until just tender. Drain well and cool.

Heat the oil over medium–high heat. Dip cauliflower florets in the batter and deep fry in the oil until tcrispy. Drain on crumpled absorbent paper.

Serves 4

CAULIFLOWER CHEESE

1 small cauliflower, cut into florets
1 tablespoon cornflour
¼ cup milk, plus extra 2 cups
½ teaspoon salt
½ cup freshly grated tasty cheese

Cook the cauliflower until just tender. Drain.

Meanwhile, mix the cornflour with ¼ cup of the milk to make a paste. In a saucepan, bring the 2 cups of milk and salt to the boil and immediately whisk in the cornflour paste, stirring constantly. Mix in the grated cheese. Carefully mix in the cooked cauliflower.

Serves 4

VARIATIONS

Cauliflower cheese bake

Transfer the cauliflower cheese into a greased casserole dish and sprinkle with ½ cup grated cheese. Bake in the oven at 180°C (350°F/gas 4) for 10 minutes or until the cheese is melted and golden.

Crumbed cauliflower

Place the cauliflower cheese in a casserole dish and cover with **curried breadcrumbs**. Bake in the oven at 180°C (350°F/gas 4) for 10 minutes.

HOT POTATO SALAD

This dish is absolutely delicious and an extremely tasty accompaniment to a meal. For a reduced-fat option, use low-fat cream and mayonnaise, reduced-fat cheese and lean bacon.

> 1kg (2lb 4oz) all-purpose potatoes, peeled and cut into
>   1.5cm (½ in) cubes
> 1 onion, peeled and finely chopped
> 125g (4½oz) lean rindless bacon, diced
> ¾ cup mayonnaise
> ½ cup pouring or thickened cream
> ½ cup freshly grated tasty cheese
> 1 tablespoon chopped parsley

Preheat the oven to 180°C (350°F/gas 4). Grease a 20cm (8in) casserole dish.

Steam the potato cubes until just tender. Drain well and transfer to the dish.

Place the onion and bacon in a small frying pan over medium heat and sauté for 5 minutes or until the onion is transparent. Remove from heat and mix in the mayonnaise and cream.

Pour the cream mixture over the potato and mix carefully. Sprinkle on the cheese. Bake for 20 minutes or until heated through and cheese is melted and golden brown.

Serve with meat dishes such as beef pot roast. At serving time, sprinkle with chopped parsley.

Serves 6

LAYERED SALAD

———o

This salad is ideal for picnics and barbecues because it can be made the day before; in fact it is preferable to do so. Unlike a lot of salads, it does not go soggy overnight.

1½ cups torn lettuce leaves
2 spring onions, finely chopped
1 cup cooked or drained tinned corn kernels
1¼ cups freshly grated tasty cheese
6 hard-boiled eggs, peeled and roughly chopped
1 cup coarsely grated carrot
3 celery stalks, thinly sliced
1 cup fresh or thawed frozen peas
½–¾ cup whole egg mayonnaise

Layer the lettuce, spring onions, corn, cheese, egg, carrot, celery and peas in a large salad bowl and top with a thin layer of mayonnaise. Cover bowl with cling wrap.

Place the salad in the fridge for at least 2 hours, or, even better, leave overnight. Serve with cold meats or chicken.

Serves 6

PAPRIKA POTATOES

500g (1lb 2oz) potatoes, peeled and cut into
    1.25cm (½in) dice
1 tablespoon light olive oil
1 onion, peeled and finely chopped
1 garlic clove, peeled and crushed
1 heaped tablespoon tomato paste
1 tablespoon paprika
½ cup pouring or thickened cream
½ cup chicken stock
3 teaspoons **tomato sauce**
1 dessertspoon cornflour mixed to a paste with a little
    cold milk

Steam the potato until just tender.

Heat the oil in a frying pan over medium heat. Add the onion and sauté for 3 minutes or until soft. Add the garlic and sauté for 1 minute. Stir in the tomato paste, paprika, cream, stock and tomato sauce and bring to the boil. Stir in some or all of the cornflour paste, if necessary, to thicken. Add the potato, mix gently and cook until heated through. Add salt and pepper to taste. Serve with grilled steak and steamed green vegetables.

Serves 4

PARSNIP MASH

———o

1kg (2lb 4oz) parsnips, peeled, any tough core discarded,
    and diced
30g (1oz) butter
2 teaspoons lemon juice
½ cup milk or pouring or thickened cream, approximately
¼ cup freshly grated tasty cheese (optional)

Cook the parsnips in a little boiling water until very tender. Drain well, return
to the pan and mash with the butter and lemon juice. Add salt and pepper to
taste. Whisk in enough milk or cream to make a smooth puree, then stir in
the grated cheese, if using. Serve with lamb dishes.

Serves 4–6

VARIATIONS

You can use carrots in this recipe in place of the parsnips. Alternatively,
you can use a combination of parsnip and carrot.

A very little **sweet chilli sauce** can be added for an interesting twist and
extra flavour.

POLENTA

———◦

Polenta can be served with a range of hot savoury dishes such as peperonata or spiced chicken with chilli yoghurt.

    2½ cups vegetable or chicken stock
    ½ cup polenta
    ½ teaspoon salt
    ½ cup freshly grated parmesan cheese

Place the stock in a saucepan over medium heat and bring to the boil. Gradually add the polenta and salt, stirring constantly, and cook for 10–12 minutes or until thickened, stirring frequently. Mix in the parmesan, season with salt and pepper and serve immediately.

Hint: *Any left-over cooked polenta can be poured into a greased 1.25cm (½ in) deep baking tin. When cold, cut into triangles or squares and shallow fry in a little olive oil and/or butter. Children generally love this, particularly if served with vegetarian pasta sauce.*

Serves 4–6

POTATO AND GARLIC MASH

1kg (2lb 4oz) all-purpose potatoes
30g (1oz) butter
1 garlic clove, crushed
½ cup milk, approximately
1 egg

Peel the potatoes and cut into 3cm (1¼in) chunks. Cook in a little boiling water until very tender. Drain well and mash until very smooth. Mix in the butter, garlic and milk, then whisk in the egg. If the mixture is still a little dry, mix in some extra milk. Season with salt and pepper. Serve with meat or poultry dishes.

Serves 6

VARIATION
Add ¼–½ cup freshly grated tasty or parmesan cheese.

POTATO BAKE

—⌁

This is a decadent dish. I don't make it often, but when I do it's always a crowd pleaser. For a reduced-fat option, use low-fat cream, low-fat cheese and lean bacon.

1kg (2lb 4oz) potatoes, peeled and thinly sliced
1½ teaspoons salt, approximately
1 onion, peeled and thinly sliced
125g (4½oz) lean rindless bacon, diced
500ml (17fl oz) pouring or thickened cream
125g (4½oz) freshly grated tasty cheese

Preheat the oven to 170°C (325°F/gas 3). Grease a 20cm (8in) casserole dish.

Layer one-third of the potato in the prepared dish, cover with half the onion, a light sprinkling of salt, then add one-third of the bacon. Drizzle one-third of the cream over the top. Repeat this layering with the potato, onion, salt, bacon and cream.

Cover with the remaining potato and cream, then sprinkle on the cheese and the remaining bacon. Bake for 1 hour or until the potatoes are tender and the top is golden brown and crispy.

Serve with meat and poultry dishes.

Serves 6

VARIATION
For individual serves, bake in 12–16 (½-cup capacity), well-greased muffin holes at 180°C (350°F/gas 4) for 20–30 minutes.

POTATO PUFFS

This is a handy recipe for using up leftover mashed potato.

45g (1¾oz) butter
½ cup water
75g (2¾oz) plain flour
1 egg
375g (13oz) leftover mashed potatoes
canola or peanut oil for frying
tomato chutney, to serve

Place the butter and water in a saucepan over medium heat and bring to the boil. Add the flour and stir with a wooden spoon until the mixture comes together and forms a ball. Reduce the heat to low and cook, stirring constantly, for 2 minutes. Remove from the heat and allow to cool for at least 10 minutes.

Whisk in the egg, then beat in the mashed potato and season with salt.

Heat the oil in a large frying pan over medium–high heat. Drop tablespoonfuls of potato mixture into the oil and cook for 3 minutes or until nicely browned. Turn and cook for a further 2–3 minutes or until other side is golden brown. Remove with a slotted spoon and drain on crumpled paper towels.

These are delicious served just with a little tomato chutney, but are also a great accompaniment to a meal, such as chicken, feta and tomato turnovers or a pot roast.

Serves 6

VARIATION

I've also made these puffs with mashed sweet potato with equally pleasing results. I haven't tried using mashed pumpkin, but see no reason why it wouldn't work.

SWEDE AND BACON CASSEROLE

750g (1lb 10oz) swede, peeled and diced
125g (4½oz) lean rindless bacon, diced
1 onion, peeled and finely chopped
1 tablespoon plain flour
1½ cups chicken or vegetable stock
¼ teaspoon dried thyme
2 tablespoons chopped parsley
pinch of dried basil

Preheat the oven on to 170°C (325°F/gas 3). Grease a 20cm (8in) casserole dish.

Cook the swede in boiling water for 7 minutes. Drain well and place in prepared casserole dish.

Meanwhile, place the bacon and onion in a small saucepan over medium heat. Sauté for 5 minutes or until the onion is transparent. Reduce the heat to low, add the flour, mix well and stir for 1 minute. Gradually add the stock and stir until the mixture comes to the boil. Simmer for 1–2 minutes, or until the sauce has thickened, then stir in the thyme, parsley and basil. Pour the sauce over the swede and stir gently to combine. Cover the casserole with a lid or foil and bake for 30 minutes or until the swede is tender.

This dish is very tasty, and is especially good as a side dish with roast beef or lamb.

Serves 6

TOMATO AND ONION GRATIN

750g (1lb 10oz) tomatoes, sliced
1 onion, peeled and sliced
2 teaspoons sugar
1 teaspoon salt
¼ teaspoon ground black pepper
1 cup fresh breadcrumbs
30g (1oz) butter, diced

Preheat the oven on to 170°C (325°F/gas 3). Grease a 20cm (8in) casserole dish.

Place a layer of the tomato in the base of prepared casserole dish, add a layer of the onion and sprinkle on a little sugar, salt and pepper. Repeat this layering process, finishing with a layer of tomato. Cover with breadcrumbs and dot with butter. Bake for 45 minutes, or until the tomatoes and onions are cooked and the topping is golden brown.

Serves 4–6

YORKSHIRE PUDDINGS

My children have always loved these 'gravy soakers', as they call them.

- 2 eggs
- 1 cup plain flour
- ½ teaspoon salt
- ½ cup milk
- ½ cup water

Preheat the oven to 210°C (415°F/gas 6–7). Grease 12 (¼-cup capacity) muffin holes.

Combine all the ingredients in a bowl and beat until smooth. Pour into the muffin holes and bake for 20–25 minutes or until puddings are puffed and golden. Do not open the oven during cooking time, if possible. Serve immediately.

These puddings are a wonderful accompaniment to roast beef.

Serves 6

SUBSTITUTIONS

I'm sure you all know the feeling of going to the cupboard and finding you lack ingredients to make whatever you had in mind. So I've put this chart together to overcome any emergency. While these substitutions are not quite the same as the real thing, they will help avoid a culinary disaster.

Ingredient required	Substitute with
Allspice (ground)	Combine ½ teaspoon ground cinnamon, ¼ teaspoon ground ginger, ¼ teaspoon ground cloves
Balsamic vinegar	Sherry or cider vinegar with a pinch of allspice per 1 cup vinegar
Beans, dried—¾ cup	425g (15oz) canned beans
Butter	Use equal amount of margarine, but not light varieties
Buttermilk	Add 2 teaspoons lemon juice to 1 cup skim milk and allow to stand for a few minutes
Caster sugar	Use food processor to grind white sugar to finer caster sugar texture
Chilli, 1 small fresh	½ teaspoon mild chilli powder

Ingredient required	Substitute with
Cornflour, for thickening	Use equal part plain flour or arrowroot
Cottage cheese	Ricotta cheese
Cream cheese	1 cup plain yoghurt drained for a few hours through a muslin-lined colander
Crème fraiche	1 cup cream + 1 tablespoon plain yoghurt. Leave to stand for a few hours at room temperature
Dijon mustard	1 tablespoon powdered mustard mixed with 1 teaspoon white wine and 1 teaspoon white, cider or white wine vinegar, 2 teaspoons mayonnaise and ¼ teaspoon sugar
Galangal	Grated fresh green ginger
Garlic—2 cloves	¼ teaspoon garlic powder or 1 teaspoon granulated garlic or a pinch of garlic salt
Ginger, ground—1 teaspoon	2 teaspoons grated fresh green ginger
Herbs, fresh—1 tablespoon	1 teaspoon dried herbs
Ketchup	1 cup tomato sauce + 1 tablespoon white, cider or white wine vinegar
Lard	Butter or vegetable oil
Lemon grass—1 stalk	2 teaspoons finely grated lemon zest
Lemon juice—1 teaspoon	½ teaspoon white wine vinegar (savoury dishes only) or 1 teaspoon lime juice or white wine

Ingredient required	Substitute with
Mascarpone—1 cup	1½ cups sieved ricotta or 200g (7oz) cream cheese whisked until smooth with ¼ cup pouring or thickened cream
Mayonnaise—1 cup	1 cup sour cream + ½ teaspoon white or cider vinegar or 1 cup plain yoghurt
Milk, fresh—1 cup	¼ cup powdered milk + ¾ cup water, or ⅔ cup evaporated milk + ⅓ cup water, or 1 cup soy or rice milk
Nutmeg	Mace
Saffron	Pinch of turmeric
Self-raising flour	For each cup plain flour, add 2 teaspoons baking powder
Sour cream	Plain yoghurt
Tomatoes—425g (15oz) tin	250g (9oz) chopped fresh tomatoes or with ½ cup water and 1 tablespoon tomato paste
Tomato juice—1 cup	Use ½ cup tomato puree with ½ cup water
Tomato paste	Cook down 1 cup tomato puree to ½ cup
Vanilla bean	1 teaspoon vanilla essence
White sugar—1 cup	¾ cup honey or 1 cup brown sugar
Wine—savoury dishes	Beef, chicken or vegetable stock
Wine—sweet dishes	Apple juice or grape juice
Yeast, dry—3 teaspoons	30g (1oz) compressed yeast

ACKNOWLEDGEMENTS

To my Tasmania listeners of the 'Jams and Preserves' talkback on ABC Local Radio for their enthusiasm for the preserving of fresh produce. To Chris Wisbey, for his appreciation for fine food and the fun in its preparation. Special thanks in recent times to Matthew Lucas, Courtney's boyfriend and the most recent conscript to our kitchen, who has become a willing and able assistant in our culinary endeavours.

ABOUT THE AUTHOR

SALLY WISE is the bestselling author of *A Year in a Bottle* and *Slow Cooker*. She is a regular guest on ABC Local Radio in Tasmania, and often holds cooking demonstrations at Gardening Australia Expos and community events. Sally loves to share the cooking experience and has taught children and adults of all ages. She is also passionate about seasonal produce and creating exciting flavours from natural, readily available ingredients.

INDEX